A
SAC

In this beautiful, informative journey through the symbolism and meaning of one of nature's loveliest flowers, Mara Freeman explores the lore of the rose and its perennial blossoming as a motif of beauty, joy, love, and secret wisdom in religion, myth, and the arts. Above all, it offers a deep dive into its archetypal relationship to both the Divine Feminine and the human soul.

Margie McArthur, author of *Faery Healing*, **and** *Lady of the Sea*, **etc., Santa Cruz, California**

Mara Freeman's life's work has been to offer seekers on the path a profound route into their personal quest. Her earlier books, *Kindling the Celtic Spirit* and *Grail Alchemy,* are two of my go-to resources for finding the depths of mystery in this world and in others. I was keen to read her latest book, *Sacred Rose: The Soul's Path to Beauty and Wisdom*. Filled with magnificent colour illustrations, and with rose-centred meditations which can be undertaken to fully illuminate the deeper messages and learning within, this book will delight any person on a spiritual quest.

Nina Milton, Author, *The Shaman Mysteries*, **etc., Rhydlewis, Wales**

This beautiful book provides the reader with a way to spiritually connect with the Rose. Mara takes you on a rose-filled journey from the beginning of time to the modern day, revealing the esoteric nature of the Rose through history, poetry, and ancient wisdom. Those interested in the mysteries of the divine feminine will not be disappointed. Highly recommended!

Annwyn Avalon, Author, *The Way of the Water Priestess*, etc., Glastonbury, England

This is a magical little book, like a Tardis; once inside you are taken on a journey of astounding breadth and depth 'from limited self to infinite consciousness': Ms Freeman follows the rose as magical and spiritual symbol throughout the breadth and depth of history, mythology and many different cultures and religions. As the lotus in Eastern traditions is a symbol of enlightenment, so the rose in the Western tradition which has its roots in the ancient Middle East and Persia, is widely seen as 'a path to spiritual realisation and also its attainment'. And in the Western tradition the rose resonates with the Grail as a symbol of the soul: 'Both these symbols suggest the receptive vessel of the soul, opening to receive divine Grace.' I have come to appreciate *Sacred Rose* as a companion: easy to carry with me, to have by my side during the meditations which follow each section, and simply to enjoy again and again.

Patricia Murphy, Editor, *De Numine,* The Journal of the Alister Hardy Trust (retired), Newcastle Emlyn, Wales

Through an illuminating exploration of the symbol of the rose throughout the West's inner and poetic traditions, Mara Freeman skilfully offers us byways to an enchanted garden where deep knowledge and spiritual realisation await. The accompanying meditations and practices allow the essence of the rose, in all its natural and metaphorical glory, a chance to permeate our minds and senses, and to bring forth our innate wisdom.

Siobhán Houston, EdD, author of *Invoking Mary Magdalene*, etc., Denver, Colorado

In this wonderful book Mara takes the reader on a journey to many traditions and cultures that have understood this queen of flowers as sacred. Each chapter contains well researched historical and sacred scripts, poetry and legend, then invites the reader to take a personal journey of discovery through rose-centred meditations, to which I return again and again. This book is beyond a knowledge of the rose to become personal experience. Highly recommended!

Janine Hartley, lecturer in Feminist Theological Studies, Melbourne, Australia

I loved reading this book and no doubt will return to it many times…I could feel the beauty of the sacred rose through the poetry, artwork and narrative. It is heart-warming in its appreciation of the rose in all its many guises, and it is soul-opening in its potential to help the reader along their spiritual path. The artwork is beautiful, as are the meditations, which will help anyone with an interest in the spiritual side of life to experience the transformational quality of the rose. For me, this book pulled together so many aspects of the sacred rose, and helped me understand the wisdom that is held within its beauty. It has been a great help to me and also a really enjoyable and compelling read.

Amanda Glynn, Chalice Well, Glastonbury, England

I have travelled over a long time down many different roads to heal myself from the wounds I have suffered. However, Mara, it is your meditations that have been so fruitful for me. The Fire of Roses meditation feels as if on a deep level I have found and own myself with clarity and light.
Elise Bernheim, LMFCC, San Jose, California

SACRED ROSE

THE SOUL'S PATH
TO BEAUTY AND WISDOM

SACRED ROSE

THE SOUL'S PATH
TO BEAUTY AND WISDOM

MARA FREEMAN

Matador
Unit E2 Airfield Business Park,
Harrison Road, Market Harborough,
Leicestershire LE16 7UL
Tel: 0116 279 2299
Email: books@troubador.co.uk
Web: www.troubador.co.uk/matador
Twitter: @matadorbooks

ISBN 978 1803136 240

British Library Cataloguing in Publication Data.
A catalogue record for this book is available from the British Library.

Printed and bound in the UK by TJ Books Limited, Padstow, Cornwall
Typeset in 11pt Aldine by Troubador Publishing Ltd, Leicester, UK

Matador is an imprint of Troubador Publishing Ltd

To the Lady of the Rose Garden

Come out here
Where the roses
Have opened.
Let soul
And world
Meet.

Rumi

CONTENTS

INTRODUCTION

INTO THE ROSE GARDEN

Mystery glows in the rose bed, the secret is hidden in the rose.
Farid ud-din Attar, 12th century

he Rose is one of the most exquisite images of spirituality in the western world: a timeless expression of beauty, wisdom, love, and, ultimately, union with the Divine. It's easy to see why: the very sensuality of the flower – its soft petals, glorious colours and heavenly scent – opens a gateway leading from this world to a higher order of reality altogether. The humble rose in the suburban garden or hedgerow becomes a radiant portal into the Mysteries of life, death and rebirth.

Like the lotus of the east, the Rose is both a symbol of the path to spiritual realisation and also its attainment. The arduous journey from limited self to infinite consciousness is suggested by the structure and growth patterns of both flowers. The lotus is rooted in thick mud through which the stem must rise and break through the surface of a lake in order to blossom in the rays of the sun. The Path of the Rose is beset by sharp and terrible thorns of earthly suffering that pierce the heart so that the soul within may be set free. Both blossoms have multi-layered circles of petals that draw us into ever deeper communion with a golden core, the still centre of the turning wheel, that is both the human soul and the Divine Presence which it seeks.

The Rose grows in the heart, unfurling one petal at a time under the life-giving rays of the Sun, the illuminating power of divine intelligence. When the Rose of the heart starts to open, we slowly awaken to the presence of Love and we see the connectedness of all created beings. The heart is the seat of the soul, the essential core of our being, and when the Rose of the soul unfolds, we open to receive the downpouring of pure Love and Light from above.

The Rose shares its symbolism with the Holy Grail, the mysterious chalice that is the other primary Western symbol of the soul. The word 'chalice' comes from the Latin word, *calyx*, meaning cup, and is the name given to the cup-like sepals of a flower that support the petals. Both these symbols suggest the receptive vessel of the soul, opening to receive divine Grace. Indeed, the symbolism of the Rose is even more complex than the Grail, given the beauty of its form, the number and arrangement of the petals with their velvety texture, the intoxicating perfume and, deep inside, the hidden golden heart enfolded within the petals, concealing the Mystery at the sacred centre of all things.

As a symbol of both time and eternity, the Rose is also a sentinel of wisdom, silence and death. The fading petals that drop like tears bear eloquent testimony to the transience of life in the physical dimension where the human heart is impaled again and again upon the thorns of loss and grief. The flower of the goddess of life is stained with the blood of Adonis and of Christ. The Roman festival of the dead was called the *Rosalia*, while in some parts of Germany, a graveyard is known as a rose-garden. Yet the presence of the Rose at death speaks of hope, the promise of rebirth, and the power of love to transcend even death itself.

THE ROSE GARDEN

The Sacred Rose can be found within the Rose Garden, a primal paradise whose archetype still resides within the human psyche as an image of lost Eden. 'Paradise' comes from the Persian word for a walled garden, so the Rose Garden is enclosed to offer respite from the profane sphere outside its walls, a sanctuary from the desert of the world. Yet to enter the rose garden requires great courage, the kind that poet T. S. Eliot called 'the awful daring of a moment's surrender which an age of prudence can never retract.' To open that door, to breach the Gates of Eden, is to risk all for love. Like Alice, we have to be willing to become very small indeed, by stripping away the usual baggage of our identity as a personality, in order to get inside.

The Sufi poets entered the garden on wings. Like the nightingale who fell in love with the Rose in Persian legend, they too poured out their deep longing to the Beloved in intoxicated songs of praise and yearning. To the medieval Christian mind, the Rose Garden became the sanctuary of the heart where the soul, like a bride, sits weaving garlands, while she awaits the coming of the divine groom and the consummation of their sacred union. The Alchemists viewed the rose garden as their laboratory for the Great Work: the gate was narrow, for only those whose lives were purified of all except divine intent could enter in. For the garden is one of the most potent symbols of the Self as a place that we constantly seek in our dreams and spiritual longings; a place where the soul can rest and be refreshed by the fountains of spirit. New and delicate seeds can be coaxed into life in the fertile soul of the heart. This too is a place of mystic marriage: a secret *temenos* in which bloom roses white and red, signifying the feminine lunar and masculine solar principles. The union of these opposites and their integration in the human psyche gives birth to the radiant spirit, often depicted as a golden rose.

When the Rose is perceived as Divine Presence itself, it becomes a symbol of cosmic order and harmony. The vast celestial white rose of the magnificent final image in Dante's *Paradiso* is an infinitely unfurling mandala, shining with the reflected Light of God that is 'the love that moves the sun and the other stars'.

Yet while we can travel to transcendental heights into the heart of the cosmic Rose, we can also retrace our steps back into the microcosm – perhaps into a quiet garden on a June evening – and experience what Eliot calls 'the moment in the rose-garden' where time and eternity are one.

THE PATH OF THE ROSE

A tradition from the Middle East alludes to a long-forgotten spiritual path known as the 'Path of the Rose'. Although we know nothing about this mysterious teaching from history, the Rose, like all potent archetypal images, is a portal that opens onto a spiritual dimension that can still be explored today by those who wish to bring more beauty and wisdom into their lives. This book is designed to open this portal for you to have a first-hand experience of the deep Mysteries of the Rose as a way of connecting with your own soul, your essence, your authentic self. In each chapter, we trace the evolution of the Rose as a sacred image throughout the ages. Each of these teachings offers a unique Path on which you can travel to experience the spiritual power and beauty of the Rose in its many aspects through a guided meditation. Through entering into the hidden wisdom of the Rose you'll be able to create your own inner Rose Garden – a haven of the heart, a sanctuary of the soul, a timeless place that you can visit over and over again for refreshment of the spirit.

CREATING SACRED SPACE

Before you begin, you may want to create a special, quiet place in your home – or perhaps in your garden, if you have one – where you can practice the meditations undisturbed. If you do them in the same place every day, a special charge builds up that makes it easier to enter sacred space every time you go there. Here are some suggestions for practical ways in which to enter more deeply into the Mysteries of the Sacred Rose, but the meditations are still as effective without them.

❖ Raise a dedicated altar: This creates a sacred centre that helps you focus on the special frequency of this work. This does not have to be anything very complicated: a small table, covered with a white cloth and a candle, (preferably made from a natural substance like beeswax or vegetable oil) will suffice.

❖ Use rose fragrance: The flower of the rose has properties that exert a powerful effect on body and mind. The 11th century Arab physician, Avicenna, was the first to distil rose oil, and wrote an entire book on the healing attributes of rose water. The essential oil is used in herbal medicine today for many physical ailments, including respiratory and skin diseases. In aromatherapy, rose calms the mind and balances the emotions, and in general creates a sense of well-being. A tea made from the flowers or hips is said to increase powers of prophecy, especially if taken before bed. Dab some rose oil, water or hydrosol on your heart or brow, or warm the oil in an aromatherapy diffuser to permeate the whole room with fragrance.

Important: Only ever use rose oil of the highest quality: The best is known as 'otto' or 'attar' of roses and is harvested in Bulgaria. Only this, or pure damask rose from the Middle East, should be used in your sacred space.

❖ Use actual roses: If you can obtain fresh roses in season, a single rose in a glass vase will add the perfect finishing touch. If that's not available, then a photograph or artwork will be fine. Spend some time gazing into the heart of the rose, breathing its fragrance, infusing your senses with its beauty, letting your consciousness become one with it. Or find a way to use dried roses in your sacred space; for example, the petals look beautiful scattered over a white cloth.

❖ Add other sacred objects: You might also feel inspired to add other resonant items, such as a piece of rose quartz, a few rosehips, or a rosary of dried rosehips – but don't clutter the altar unnecessarily: it should have a simple, serene feeling that enables you to slip into a sacred state of mind as soon as you sit before it. It's highly recommended to keep a journal of your experiences on the Path of the Rose. You may be surprised at the further insights and revelations that can emerge as you record your meditation.

And now… I invite you to take a walk through the Rose Garden with me.

CHAPTER ONE

A GARLAND FOR A GODDESS

On her hair she wears a garland of sweet-smelling roses,
and ever she sends the Loves to assist in the court of wisdom.
Euripides, Medea[1]

he Rose, as the flower of love and beauty, belongs to the Great Goddess. With its scented, folded petals that slowly unfurl, revealing its secret heart as it opens to receive the rays of the sun, it speaks of the feminine principle and the eternal mystery of the continuity of life. From antiquity the Canaanites and Phoenicians scattered rose petals over the altars of Ashtoreth, while the Corybantes, the wild, dancing priests of Cybele, the Phrygian earth goddess, cast the flowers at her image as it was borne in procession. In Egypt it held pride of place as the flower of Isis. In ancient Greece, the rose belonged to Aphrodite, goddess of love and life and the fecundity of the natural world. The plant was not native to Greece and it is not known when it first came

1

there. The well-travelled historian, Herodotus, believed it was first brought to Greece by Midas, whose rose garden in Macedonia was world famous for its beauty and fragrance. It was certainly cultivated in Asia Minor and Greece during the 7th century BCE. However, the oldest writers believed it first grew on the island of Cythera, renowned for its cult of Aphrodite. In this chapter we will explore the Rose as the primary flower of these goddesses of the ancient world.

APHRODITE'S FLOWER

Aphrodite was not a native Greek goddess. She migrated there from the Near East where she was a close relative of life-giving goddesses such as Ishtar and Astarte, and the Sumerian Inanna, who, like Aphrodite's Roman counterpart, was synonymous with the planet Venus, the morning and evening star. Her cult dates back to the 8th century BCE when she was called Kypros, goddess of the island of Cyprus. Aphrodite embodies the beauty of the rose that opens the heart to joy. The poet Hesiod tells us that wherever she roamed, new life sprang up and the flame of love was kindled in every heart.

In Hesiod's creation myth, Aphrodite was born of the union of Heaven (Ouranos) and Earth (Gaia), albeit in an unconventional way. When Heaven folded himself around Earth in a loving embrace at night, one of their sons, Chronos, (Time) castrated his father with a sickle, and the severed genitals fell into the sea as swirling white foam. The waves swept the foam along the coast of the island of Cythera and into Cyprus, where the beautiful young goddess emerged, as from the primordial ocean of life.

About them a white foam grew from the immortal flesh, and in it a girl formed.

First she approached holy Cythera, then from there she came to sea-girt Cyprus. And out stepped a modest and beautiful goddess, and the grass began to grow all round beneath her slender feet. Gods and men call her Aphrodite, because she was formed in foam, and Cytherea, because she approached Cythera, and Cyprus-born, because she was born in wave-washed Cyprus, and 'genial', because she appeared out of genitals. Eros and fair Desire attended her birth and accompanied her as she went to join the family of gods.[2]

Another version tells how when she rose from the waves, the seafoam turned into white roses to cover her nakedness. This story may have its origins in an earlier myth of the Hindu goddess, Lakshmi, who was birthed from the sea itself. Lakshmi was born from the churning foam of the primordial ocean, the 'Ocean of Milk'. Like Aphrodite, she is a goddess of love and beauty, and in one version of her origin myth she was born from a rose.

As Aphrodite stepped ashore, the goddesses known as the Graces and the Hours – the seasons of the year – marvelled at her exquisite beauty and welcomed her with joy. They clothed her with garments they had made for her, dyed with spring flowers: crocuses, hyacinths, violets, narcissus and lily, and – of course – the 'rose's lovely bloom'. Wherever the foam fell to the ground, white rose bushes grew, and as she walked, the earth blossomed under her feet. One of her epithets was *Aphrodite en Kepois* (in the gardens) and the poet of the *Cypria* paints an idyllic picture of her in springtime:

Then laughter-loving Aphrodite and her handmaidens
wove sweet-smelling crowns of the flowers of the earth and
put them upon their heads – bright-coiffed goddesses, the
Nymphs and Graces, and golden Aphrodite too, while they
sang sweetly on the Mount of many-fountained Ida.[3]

In the provinces of Corinth and Mantinea, a 'black Aphrodite' presided over the richly fertile 'black earth' and was also associated with the powers of the night, characteristics she shares with Black Isis.

In Greek society she was called upon for her power over relationships of all kinds, drawing people together in harmony, sanctifying their union, and ensuring healthy offspring for the continuity of the community. Plato, in his *Symposium*, gave her two names: Aphrodite Ourania, the celestial goddess of spiritual love, and Aphrodite Pandemos, common Aphrodite, who presided over weddings and marriage. Brides-to-be made sacrifices at her temple the night before their wedding, praying for her to grant them a happy marriage and bless them with children. She was equally important to courtesans and prostitutes who played an integral role in Greek society.

Her sacred flower graced every aspect of their lives, especially in customs that celebrated love. Lovers hung garlands of roses on their beloveds' door and the bridal wreath was also made from them. Lovers lay together on beds strewn with roses, inhaling their heavenly fragrance on pillows filled with petals.

The Birth of Aphrodite, sometimes called *The Return of the Maiden,*
marble, *c. 470 – 460 BCE,* Ludovisi Throne
Every year in her temple at Paphos in Cyprus, Aphrodite's
handmaidens bathed and dressed her in the garments of Spring.

SHADOWY WITH ROSES

In early Greece, garlands of roses, rose oils and creams
were used lavishly in all different kinds of ceremonies and
rites of passage, especially those where love was celebrated.
In her temples, Aphrodite's devotees wore garlands of
roses upon their heads, laid them as offerings upon her
shrines, and crowned her statues with them, heightening
the senses with their beauty and fragrance. Her temple on
Paphos was connected to the seashore by a processional
way through bowers of roses and others of her sacred
flowers. Her priestesses wore wreaths of white roses, and
one of their devotions included the traditional custom
of carrying her statue to the waves for a ritual cleansing

The Birth of Venus, Sandro Botticelli (1444-1510)
The goddess floats to shore on a seashell as gentle breezes caress
her with a shower of roses. She is greeted by the Hour of Spring,
who wears a myrtle wreath about her neck and a rose girdle.

at winter's end, to celebrate her rebirth in the spring. A major temple to Aphrodite, dated to the 3rd century BCE, has also been found on the island of Rhodes, which takes its name from the Greek word for rose, *rhodon,* because of its abundance of roses. One of the island's presiding deities was Aphrodite's daughter, Rhoda.

The poet Sappho, who lived on the island of Lesbos around 600 BCE, was the first poet to celebrate the rose, evoking its beauty and association with love in many of her verses. She was the leader of a religious community of young women, known as a *thiasos,* which was devoted to the worship of Aphrodite through music, dance and song. A fragment which has survived on a shard of tile seems to be a ritual invocation petitioning the goddess to leave her cult centre on the island of Crete to join her devotees in their open-air temple:

Come to me from Crete, to your sacred temple
of delightful apple groves,
and altars fragrant with the sweet-smelling smoke of
*   frankincense.*

Within, cold water resounds through the apple boughs,
and all the place is shadowy with roses,
and a dreamless sleep falls
from the shimmering leaves.

And there is a lovely meadow blooming with flowers of
   springtime,
where breezes gently blow;
Aphrodite takes up her wreaths
and into golden cups
gracefully pours nectar, mingled with joy.

It's possible that these lines are describing an actual ritual in which a priestess, magically invoking the presence of the goddess within herself, dispenses a drink that represents nectar, the divine drink of the gods. Perhaps she has received their offerings of flower garlands or is taking them up to place on the heads of her worshippers.

How the Rose was Created

One Greek myth tells how the gods created the rose.
Chloris, the goddess of flowers, (later called Flora by the
Romans), found the dead body of a nymph in the woods
and turned her into a flower. She called upon Aphrodite,
goddess of love, who gave the flower beauty, and Dionysus,
the god of wine, who added nectar for sweet fragrance. Then
Zephyr, god of the West Wind, blew the clouds away so
that Apollo, the sun god, could shine and make it bloom.
Chloris declared it to be the Queen of Flowers,
and so the rose came into being.

Detail from a fresco in Villa Arianna, Stabiae, Napoli
*As she talks, her lips breathe spring roses: I was Chloris, who am now
called Flora.* – Ovid [4]

The Rose is a flower of both love and death, the evanescence of life and the sorrow of bereavement. The flower whose petals fade all too soon, whose thorns are razor sharp, is a reminder of the unbearable pain of separation as well as the ecstasy of union. This was the chosen flower of the slain god Dionysus, whose initiates wore garlands of roses at his festivals. And when the dead journeyed to the underworld, they were likely to encounter Hecate, goddess of the crossroads, crowned with a wreath of five-petalled roses. In some stories the red rose was born out of pain and wounding, its thorns piercing Aphrodite's feet as she ran through the forest, or springing from her tears as she held the lifeless body of her slain lover, Adonis, whose blood stained red the wild white roses. In the Iliad, Homer describes Aphrodite in the Trojan War, anointing the dead body of the warrior hero, Hector, with rose oil.

The blossoms and oil were used in funeral rites in the classical world. In Rome, the family of one who had recently died anointed the body with aromatic oils and placed a rose upon the forehead. A vessel containing the essential oil of roses and other perfumes was buried along with the body, and flowers were strewn or planted on the grave. The poet Propertius wrote, 'If someone were to lay my body in soft rose petals, the earth would be light for me.' Thus the beloved dead, accompanied by the flower of immortality, embarked upon their journey to the Elysian Fields, where, according to the poet, Tibullus, 'the beneficent earth blooms with fragrant roses'.

Sacred Geometry: The Rose of Venus

*The flowers and fruit of the rose have an underlying fivefold
geometry. To the Pythagoreans, the number five symbolised
the conjoining of the four elements: Earth, Water, Fire,
Air, plus Ether, the living spirit which animated them.
They viewed the five-pointed star, or pentagram, as a symbol
of divine perfection, and chose it as their chief symbol of
health, wholeness and blessing. The pentagram also gives
rise to the Golden Proportion, the underlying structure of
many natural forms in the universe and found in ancient art
and music throughout the world.*

*Aphrodite was known to the Romans as Venus, who gives
her name to the bright planet that hangs like a jewel in
the sky at dawn or dusk. The orbit of the planet Venus
in relation to the Earth traces the pattern of a five-
petalled rose. Every eight years into this dance of exquisite
mathematical precision, Venus appears to touch the Earth
to form another 'petal'.*

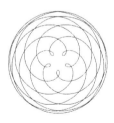

The Orbit of Venus as viewed from Earth

The rose was also the sacred flower of Isis, the greatest goddess of the ancient world. From 3000 BCE, she was worshipped in Egypt as Queen of Heaven, Lady of the House of Life, and mother of all creation. Ruler of Earth, Sky, and Underworld, she caused the sun to rise and set, and sailed forth in radiant splendour as the moon. She lavished all nature's gifts upon her human children and spread her outstretched wings over them on the journey towards death. In the Age of the Pharaohs, the lotus was the special flower of Isis. But with the arrival of the Greeks, the rose replaced the lotus in the garden of the goddess.

Isis was both sister and wife to the god, Osiris, who was murdered and dismembered by his jealous brother Set. Isis wandered the Earth, beside herself with grief, in search of fragments of his body. When she at last found them, she restored Osiris to life with her magic powers, and they conceived the god Horus. Osiris became god of the underworld and receiver of the souls of the dead. Isis gave birth to Horus who eventually became the ruler of Egypt, thanks to his mother's devotion and healing powers. When he grew up, Horus avenged his father by defeating Set in combat. Temples were dedicated to her throughout Egypt, the most important being at Philae, where her myth was re-enacted at the yearly inundation of the Nile. The tears of sorrowing Isis caused the Nile to overflow and Osiris was reborn as living water, while Horus emerged to regenerate the land. Dark rich mud oozed over the fields, turning the soil into black gold to fertilise the crops and feed her people. She held the mysteries of birth, life and death, and so they turned to her for wisdom, healing and protection, often imploring her aid for a child or family member as if for Horus himself. The roses that families placed in the coffins of their dead would therefore symbolise Isis' powers of regeneration and the hope that their beloved one, like Osiris, would be reborn in the life beyond.

Roses came to Egypt when Alexander the Great introduced Greek culture in the 4th century BCE. The Greeks planted roses all along the banks of the Nile, and in Egypt's perfect climate they were soon flourishing in gardens everywhere. Thriving industries sprang up, making oils, perfumes and incense from the petals, many of which were exported to Rome. The rose replaced the lotus, once the official flower of Egypt, in all the wreaths and garlands used to decorate temples and worn by the participants. Like many other countries throughout time, they were used lavishly in funerary rites, perhaps because their heavenly beauty transcends death. Archaeologists have discovered tombs with paintings of roses on their walls, and rose oil was one of the ingredients used in the mummification of the body. Wreaths of roses were placed on the mummy to 'celebrate a just life, full of love towards the gods and one's neighbour.'[5] They were sometimes placed on the decorated coffin itself, as

Egyptian woman's mummy mask with a wreath of flowers, circa 100 BCE

in the case of the second coffin of Tutankhamen.[6] According-ing to the *Egyptian Book of the Dead*, as the crown was placed upon the head, a ritual text, possibly a prayer or a charm, was recited over the body.

In 1888, British archaeologist, Sir Flinders Petrie, excavated the Hawara tomb in the Fayum province of Lower Egypt, and discovered coffins decorated with figures of the goddesses, Isis and Neb-hât, whose name means 'the Lady of the House'. On one coffin there was an image of the deceased approaching the goddesses with offerings. The mummified corpse was adorned with rose wreaths upon the head and garlands on the chest. The roses were still in bud, which kept them intact and they were still perfectly preserved when Flinders found them. They were found to be the species known as *Rosa richardii* or *rosa sancta,* the Holy Rose, which have single, five-petalled blooms of pale pink and can still be found in many sacred gardens of the Middle East. They date back to about 170 CE and are the oldest recorded samples of a rose species that still exists today.

Petrie described the miraculous way the roses appeared to come back to life:

> *In the dry desert air, the wreath's petals had shrivelled, but still kept their colour, and when placed in warm water, the blossoms seemed to come back to life. Buds swelled, and the pink petals spread unfolding to reveal a knot of golden threads at the centre just as they had been on the morning of the funeral.* [7]

ISIS IN GREECE AND ROME

The fame of Isis spread far beyond the Nile. As 'Isis of the Many Names', she spread her wings that turned into sails and voyaged forth across the Mediterranean to become Queen of Heaven and Earth in the Greco-Roman world. By the 2nd century BCE, Isis had become enormously popular, and she was easily assimilated into Hellenistic culture. Temples dedicated to her worship sprang up in Athens, Rome and other cities, and festivals such as the *Rhodophoria* ('the festival of bearing roses') and *Rosalia* or *Rosaria,* were held from May to July. Devotees of Isis and other goddesses of fertility, such as Aphrodite and Demeter, held processions in which they adorned themselves and statues of their deities with wreaths and garlands of roses. As well as being a time to celebrate fertility and new life, the Rosalia was also a festival of those who had recently died, whose tombs were lovingly decorated with roses, in hopes for their immortality.

THE GOLDEN ASS

We can catch a glimpse of what went on in this mystery religion in the Roman novel, *Metamorphoses*, or *The Golden Ass*, written by Lucius Apuleius, a travelling lawyer and orator from North Africa, born around 125 CE. A Platonic philosopher, Apuleius was also deeply interested in magic and religion, and in a previous work recounted how he had participated in many sacred rites and ceremonies. The novel is a veiled account of a journey of initiation into the mystery religion of Isis, of which Apuleius himself was most likely an initiate. And perhaps we shouldn't be too surprised that the story hinges upon a bunch of roses!

Although it is a long and rambling tale with many intricate subplots and digressions, the main thread is as follows:

Photis promises to help
Lucius the Ass

A young Roman businessman named Lucius is travelling through Greece and arrives in Thessaly, an area famous for witchcraft and magic. He stays at the home of the wealthy Milo, whose wife, Pamphile, is reputed to be a notorious witch. Lucius is fascinated by everything to do with magic, and secretly hopes to become the witch's apprentice. He seduces her maidservant, Photis, in order to spy on Pamphile at her magic. Photis agrees to help him and arranges a time when he can secretly watch Pamphile turn herself into an owl in order to fly to her lover. Lucius is fascinated by this and begs Photis to show him how to work the same magic on himself. However, she gives him the wrong potion, and instead of a bird, he turns into an ass. The owl is a symbol of wisdom, but Lucius has turned into the proverbial animal of stupidity.

Photis reassures Lucius that she can easily restore him to his human shape by giving him the antidote in the form of a bunch of roses. But, before she can fetch one, bandits break into the house and steal Milo's gold, which they load onto the ass's back to haul it to their hideout in a cave. By the time Lucius is eventually rescued from the bandits, the season for roses is over. He ends up being passed from one owner to another, suffering much cruelty and humiliation. Whenever he seems to be within reach of roses, something happens to prevent him from taking them. The final blow comes when he learns he is to have sexual intercourse with a female criminal in a public amphitheatre. He manages to escape and gallops for his life to a hidden spot on the seashore, where he falls asleep, exhausted, in a sandy hollow.

Just before midnight he awakens, startled to see the full moon rising over the sea, shining with a strange otherworldly brilliance. In this numinous atmosphere, Lucius ardently invokes the goddess to take pity on him and return him to his human shape. Isis herself emerges from the sea in all her majestic glory and answers his prayer. She tells him to attend the ceremony being held in her honour on the following day. She will instruct the priest in a dream to carry a garland of roses. Lucius must join the procession, approach the priest and under the pretence of kissing his hand, take a bite of the roses, at which point he will become human again. In return he must pledge to devote the rest of his life to her service. All goes according to plan, and to his great joy and the amazement of the crowd, Lucius is restored to his human shape. He follows the procession to the temple of Isis and works as a temple servant until the goddess indicates that he is ready for initiation. He undergoes three elaborate and profound initiations culminating in his ordination into the priesthood of Isis and Osiris in Rome.

While the rituals of Isis' mysteries remain unknown, we do know that initiation involved a passage from symbolic death to rebirth through the mediation of the goddess, leading to revelations and divine secrets. In *Metamorphoses,* it's highly significant that the name of its protagonist, Lucius, means light, from the Latin, *lux,* and as so often in the human condition, the light within is obscured by the search to gratify sensual desires. His impulse to gain psychic powers is encouraged by Photis, whose name also comes from the Greek word for light. His love for the pretty girl prefigures his later devotion to Isis, just as his desire to turn into a bird flying freely in the skies presages the release of his spirit from the bondage of matter. But there are no shortcuts on the spiritual path: Lucius is transformed instead into a creature whose life is one of earthbound misery. Moreover the ass had an ignominious reputation in Apuleius's time, since it was a symbol of the evil god Set, who murdered Osiris. His fall into the depths of bestiality utterly destroys his ego, and only when he is thoroughly

brought to his lowest ebb is he ready to regain his human nature and offer himself in service to the goddess. By eating the roses, he is ingesting the qualities of life, love and beauty that Isis represents. As a symbol of regeneration and immortality, they mark his initiatory rebirth and awakening to his true nature as a being of Light, the meaning of his name, through the blessing of the Great Goddess.

Marble statue of the goddess Isis with sistrum found at Hadrian's Villa, Tivoli, 2nd century, CE

The Secret Rose

Ceiling boss with Rose and Sword

The phrase, 'under the rose', refers to the ancient custom of hanging a rose over a council table to indicate that everything discussed was to remain secret. In 16th and 17th century Europe it was customary to paint or carve a rose on the ceiling of council chambers and banqueting halls for the same reason, and the motif was placed over confessional boxes in Catholic churches. Many Victorian houses still feature an ornamental plaster rose in the middle of the ceiling and it is also a modern legal term. Yet to be born 'sub rosa' also meant being illegitimate, for the wild rose was also the symbol of illicit love.

This custom may have originated in an ancient Egypt image of Horus, the divine son of Isis, whom the Greeks called Harpocrates. He was pictured sitting within a rose, his finger on his lips, commanding silence about the Mysteries. This word comes from the ancient Greek schools of initiation, where the word used was mysterion from the verb myein, 'to close', referring to the closing of the eyes or the lips. Closing the eyes referred to the withdrawal of the senses from outer reality in order to experience the inner worlds. Closing the lips referred to the vows of silence taken by the initiate, (mystes, plural mystai), regarding what took place at the sacred ceremonies, to keep them from being profaned.

The Rose both reveals and conceals; it indicates that divine wisdom is obtainable, that esoteric schools exist to help the seeker walk upon the Path, but the essence of the teaching remains hidden under and within the symbol. Only in silence and inner peace may the listening soul hear the Voice of the Divine; and then no words can adequately describe the experience.

MEDITATION I – A VISION OF ISIS

This meditation takes you to a seashore in ancient Greece, where the goddess addresses you in the same words she spoke to Lucius in the Golden Ass. This is such a vivid, poetic speech that it may have been taken from the script of an actual ritual that Apuleius himself experienced during his own temple initiations – or perhaps he wrote it to describe his own vision of Isis.

Close your eyes and take some long, slow, deep breaths, letting go of all outer concerns. Let your consciousness sink down and down into silence, then gradually start to become aware of the faint sound of waves. Opening your inner vision, you find yourself on the sandy beach of the Mediterranean Sea where little waves are lapping the shore. You have brought with you a garland of roses. A full moon is hiding behind a little cloud and the night air is soft and cool. You perform a ritual ablution by removing all your clothes, walking into the waves, and dipping into the water seven times to cleanse and purify yourself. You now cast the garland of roses as far as you can into the inky blackness. Returning to the shore, you gaze out over the calm expanse of the sea. Suddenly the moon emerges from the cloud in all its brilliance, and the figure of a radiantly beautiful goddess rises from the waves, shaking herself free of water, shining in the light of the moon as she stands poised on the surface of the waves.

Her long thick hair falls in tapering ringlets on her white neck, and she is crowned with an intricate garland woven with every kind of fruit and flower. Upon her brow gleams a round disc like a mirror, or the bright face of the moon itself. The disc is fastened with coiled vipers on either side of her head, and next to them, golden ears of wheat.

Her gown is of the finest linen, gleaming pure white, crocus-yellow, and rose red. Along its hem a woven border of flowers and fruit lifts gently in the breeze. Over the gown she wears a gleaming jet-black mantle, hung from the left shoulder, knotted at the breast, and sweeping over her right hip. Its many folds drape gracefully over her body, ending in a shimmering tasselled fringe. Sparkling stars are embroidered all over it, and in the centre glows a full moon breathing fiery rays.

In her right hand she holds a bronze sistrum, which rings out in a triple beat when she shakes the handle. A boat-shaped gold vessel hangs from her left hand; along its handle writhes a coiled asp, throat puffed out and head raised. Her lovely feet are clothed with slippers of palm leaves, the emblem of victory. The fragrance of all the perfumes of Arabia float towards you as the Goddess turns to address you in a celestial voice:

'I am Nature, the universal Mother, Mistress of all the Elements, Primordial Daughter of Time, Sovereign of all Things Spiritual, Queen of the Dead, Queen also of the Immortals, the Single Manifestation of all living Gods and Goddesses. My will commands the shining heights of heaven, the life-giving winds, the deep waters and the fertile earth. I am the Eternal Ocean from which all life pours forth and to which it all returns to be made anew. With a single gesture I command the shining heights of Heaven, the health-giving sea-breezes, and the deep silence of the Underworld. Though I am worshipped in many aspects, known by countless names, and propitiated with all manner of rites, yet the whole round earth venerates me. I am known as Aphrodite, Artemis, Demeter, Juno, and many more names, but the Egyptians call me by my true name: Queen Isis.'

Awed by her ineffable beauty and power, you fall to your knees on the sand, and raising both arms in supplication, send forth a heartfelt prayer to the Mother of Life . . . .

23

Queen Isis may respond to your prayer by speaking words to you in your mind, or she may cast a gift into the waters at your feet. You listen carefully and take the gift into your hands and raise your eyes ready to give her thanks – but she is already gone, and only the moon can be seen riding high over the waves against the midnight sky.

Seated on the sand, you spend a few moments contemplating the meaning of the gift you received. Then after a while, you start to become aware of your physical body again, and return fully to present-time consciousness, remembering all that took place on that other shore.

Spend a few moments writing about the gift you received from the goddess and what it means to you.

CHAPTER TWO

THE CELESTIAL ROSE

Mary is the soul that is a garden and the bride in the garden, the
bride of God who gives birth to God, and ever and again the Rose.
– Eithne Wilkins[8]

hat place was there for the sacred Rose when the goddesses of antiquity were banished from Western society? In the early days of Christian Europe, flowers were banned from both churches and public places, because they were associated with Roman pleasure-seeking and pagan ceremonies. Decorating a statue with crowns or garlands of flowers was forbidden, as it smacked of idolatry, not to mention the Egyptian magical practice of animating a statue with a spirit or deity. Even bridal wreaths at weddings were suspect because of their connection with pagan feasts.[9]

At the same time, the art of creating gardens was almost lost in Europe. The affluent classes whose gardens once adorned their lavish homes and temples had melted away,

25

and the hordes of barbarian invaders had little time for horticulture. With the collapse of the Roman Empire in the West, flowers that had once brought such a spirit of beauty and delight into all aspects of cultural and religious life, withered away in abandoned gardens and likewise in art and literature. They had no place in the ascetic worldview of a religion which condemned the physical world as inferior to the heavenly one. Roses came in for particularly strong censure because of their former association with Venus and also because prostitutes were forced to wear them as a mark of disgrace in ancient Rome. The goddess of love and life adorned with a circlet of blooming roses could not have stood more in contrast with the dying god bleeding from a crown of thorns.

But a flower whose beauty and fragrance are rooted so deeply in the human heart and mind could not be exiled forever. By the fourth century the church fathers revoked their ban on the rose, and declared it to be perfect among flowers, and so it became one of the most important of all Christian symbols. The influential bishop, Saint Ambrose, declared that the rose originally grew in Eden without thorns. When Adam and Eve were expelled from the garden, God gave it thorns to show they no longer lived in a perfect world, although its loveliness remained to remind the human race of their origins in Paradise.

With this ecclesiastical blessing, roses began to appear in monastery gardens, which, by the 8th century, were becoming very popular due to the influence of the Moors in southern Spain and Sicily, and later of crusaders returning from the Middle East. These sacred gardens were often conceived as a cloistered quadrangle with a central fountain

From *Tacuinum Sanitatis*, a 14th century handbook published in Italy on health and wellbeing, physical, mental and spiritual, based on living in harmony with nature and the seasons.

or small tree, and a lawn divided into four to denote the rivers flowing from Eden. Their blossoms adorned altars on special feast-days, while flower and fruit were prized for their medicinal benefits. By the 12th century the rose garden had become the standard image of paradise, while the rose became known as 'a messenger of the garden of souls'.

Roses reached their height of popularity in the 12th and 13th centuries. By this time they had regained pride of place in both cultural and religious activities from birth to burial.

Basins of rosewater were used for baptism, while garlands of roses adorned the bride and her wedding guests at marriage ceremonies. Young women who joined a nunnery to become 'brides of Christ' were also honoured in this way. In the 15th century procession of Corpus Christi in the city of Venice, children strewed rose petals on the church floor, choirboys bore vessels of rose oil, and priests carried vases of rose petals. [10] When the new bishop was installed at St Paul's Cathedral in London in 1405, both he and the canons wore garlands of red roses just like their early Roman counterparts. The Roman festival of roses, the *dies rosae,* became the church festival of Whitsuntide. Once again roses featured in burial customs, as they did in Egyptian, Greek and Roman times: monastic graveyards were planted with roses as if to prefigure the Paradise to which the souls had departed, recalling the Roman *Rosalia* festival of the dead.

Over the centuries, the rose once again became associated with Divine Love, as in earlier times. Christ was named the *flos dei,* (flower of God), who sacrificed himself for the love of mankind. The five-petalled rose of medieval Europe became a reminder of the five wounds he suffered on the cross. Its thorns were woven into the crown placed upon his head, while in some devotional allegories, the cross was depicted as the rose-bush itself.[11] Like the slain god Adonis before him, the blood of Christ was said to have stained white roses red, and in some devotional texts, his wounds were even called roses.[12] Red roses also symbolised the blood of Christian martyrs that was shed for his sake. By contrast, the yellow rose denoted the triumph of the resurrection. This gave rise to the tradition of the Golden Rose, a costly ornament made of pure gold and filled with precious incense, which the Pope gave annually to an important public figure, city, or church. The ceremony is continued today on Rose Sunday, the fourth Sunday of Lent, as a sign of hope and joy in the middle of the season of penitence.

ROSE WITHOUT A THORN

But above all, the rose became the special flower of Christ's mother, Mary, just as it had been for her predecessors in the ancient world. A direct and unbroken line can be clearly traced from the goddess religions of antiquity to the reverence paid to Mary in the Middle Ages. Many devotional pagan practices dedicated to a loving mother goddess were transferred to her as the mother of Jesus Christ.[13] Like Cybele, she was a virgin mother, and like Isis, she became known as the Mother of God and Queen of Heaven. Images of Mary with the child Jesus closely resemble those of the rose-wreathed Isis nurturing her son, Horus, while sculptures depicting the Virgin Mary cradling his dead body have their origins in Isis mourning Osiris.

Although the orthodox position of the Church was that Mary was merely 'the temple of God, not the Lord of the temple', in the popular mind, Christ's mother was of no less importance than the Magna Mater whose cult she replaced in Rome.[14] Churches dedicated to Mary were built over pagan sanctuaries: the basilica of Santa Maria sopra Minerva keeps alive the memory of Minerva, the Roman goddess of wisdom, whose temple once stood on this spot, along with an Iseum. The great church of Santa Maria Maggiore on the Esquiline Hill was erected on the site of the temple of Cybele, close to the temple of Juno Lucina, protector of pregnant mothers. Rose petals lined the path of processions honouring Mary, Mother of God, just as they were in pagan Roman festivals to the Magna Mater. In the medieval church festival of the Madonna of the Snows, white rose petals were showered down upon the congregation from the chapel ceiling, as in the feasts of pagan Rome, only now they symbolised the descent of the Holy Spirit. This practice was continued as late as the middle of the 19th century at Messina, Sicily. Perhaps we should not be surprised that the flower of the goddesses of beauty, love and divine Mystery was passed down to her Christian counterpart.

Bernard of Clairvaux, who was deeply devoted to Mary, associated her with the white rose of virtue, virginity, and love of God, and the red rose of charity, spirituality, and the extinction of vice. Red roses also became the symbol of her sorrows, as they had once been for Aphrodite, only now they owed their colour to drops of Christ's blood spilling on a thorn bush. White roses signified Mary's joy and her

(Opposite:) *The Little Garden of Paradise* by a 15th century artist known as the Upper Rhenish Master portrays the Virgin Mary surrounded by a gathering of saints from many eras. To her right, Saint Dorothy is reaching for a cherry, Saint Barbara is drawing water from a well, and Saint Cecilia holds a psaltery for the Child Jesus to pluck the strings. At the feet of Saint George there is a small dead dragon, and at those of Archangel Michael, a small black demon. Saint Oswald is leaning against a tree trunk. Many species of birds are depicted in realistic detail, while the plants and flowers were well-known mediaeval symbols of Mary.

31

purity, and the golden rose her radiant glory. The five petals proclaimed her Five Joys and the five letters of her name, MARIA. Rose garlands and wreaths were hung on church statues of Mary during her special month of May which was dedicated to her purity and love, as it was once the 'merry month' of pagan goddesses of the spring. So similar were these devotions to the female deities of old, that in 440 CE, Isidore of Pelusium warned: 'We should really be more careful in marking the difference between the heathen Magna Mater and our Magna Mater, Mary.'[15]

Mary was given many rose names throughout her medieval cult: Rose of Sharon, the Rose-garland, the Wreath of Roses, and Queen of the Most Holy Rose-Garden. In the Litany of Loreto, a prayer which appeals to Mary to intercede with God since she stands nearer to him than those who pray, she is called 'Rosa Mystica', the Mystic Rose. She was often addressed as the 'Rose without a Thorn', because she was as pure as the original rose that grew in the Garden of Eden. Because thorns appeared only when it was planted on Earth after Adam and Eve were expelled from the garden, Mary was regarded as a 'second Eve' whose purity restored her to the paradise from which Eve had been driven. As early as the 5th century CE, the poet Sedulius wrote:

As blooms among the thorns the lovely Rose,
herself without a thorn,
The glory of the bush whose crown she is,

So, springing from the root of Eve, Mary the new Maiden
Atoned for the sin of that first Maiden long ago. [16]

Mary as the rosebush gives birth to Christ, the rose. She is also a central figure in the Tree of Jesse, the genealogical tree of Christ depicted in many stained-glass church windows as a winding vine growing from the side of Jesse, father of King David. In some cases, the vine motif fuses with the rose-bush.[17] The same idea lies behind the 15th century German Christmas carol, *Es ist ein Ros entsprungen,* which translates into the well-known English version:

Lo, how a Rose e'er blooming
From tender stem hath sprung!
Of Jesse's lineage coming
As men of old have sung;
It came, a flower bright,
Amid the cold of winter
When half-gone was the night.

At the Council of Ephesus in 431 CE, Mary was said to enclose the whole of heaven and earth in her womb within the space of a single round rose, a beautiful image that later found expression in a 15th century poem:

There is no rose of such vertu
As is the rose that bare Jesu,
Alleluia.

For in this rose conteined was
Heaven and earth in littel space,
Res miranda...[18]

A 16th century text makes the simple yet profound analogy between the beauty and receptivity of the Rose and the divine spirit which is poured into it:

> *As in the morning the Rose opens, receiving the dew from heaven and the sun,*
> *so Mary's soul did open and receive Christ the heavenly dew.*[19]

As Teresa Mclean concludes in her book, *Medieval English Gardens:*

> *It was the doctrine of her motherhood that first inspired devotion to her as the Mystical Rose, and it was the doctrine of the Virgin Birth that expanded Mary's rose symbolism into the most important, complex and elaborate motif of medieval art and literature, both sacred and profane.*[20]

QUEEN OF THE ROSE GARDEN

Gardens and bowers dedicated to Mary were particularly popular in the Middle Ages and gave rise to the fashion of 'Mary Gardens', which were planted with every flower and plant that could be attributed to the Virgin. Many of these plants had previously been held sacred to goddesses such as Juno, Venus, and Diana, as well as to Hulda and Frigga of northern mythology. Mary's flowers included anemones, tulips, narcissi, violets, lilies, marigolds, primroses and stock, but the rose, of course, took pride of place. St. Benedict is known to have had a monastic rose garden, or 'rosary', in the 4th century, but the first reference to a garden dedicated to Mary is from the life of St. Fiacre, the 7th century Irish patron saint of gardening, who planted a garden of flowers with spiritual symbolism around the oratory to Our Lady at his hospice in France for the poor and infirm.[21] These gardens became even more popular when flowers were regarded as having significant healing properties in medieval medicine. Mary herself became regarded as a healer of both body and soul, and in the 14th century the fragrance of her roses, intensified in a small walled garden, was considered particularly efficacious against the plague which was ravaging Europe at the time.

This theme became a popular subject in religious art, especially in the 15th century. In these paintings Mary is pictured in an enclosed garden, sitting in a rose arbour or surrounded by a protective hedge of red and white roses: red for the Passion of Christ, and white for the Virgin's purity. She is usually shown holding the Christ child on her lap, or else he is playing nearby. More often than not, she is accompanied by angels and there may be one or more female saints nearby. The womb-like garden is a symbol of Mary herself as the Mother of God: the *hortus conclusus,* or enclosed garden in which the Holy Child was planted. This popular theme, which expresses the mystery of the Incarnation, seems to have had its origins in the Song of Songs, an erotic dialogue between a bride and groom, in which the garden becomes a metaphor for the Beloved:

She is a garden enclosed,
My sister, my promised bride;
A garden enclosed,
A sealed fountain. . . (4.12)

In verses brimming over with sensual imagery, the poem describes a garden watered by living springs, where intoxicating flowery scents are wafted by fragrant breezes:

> *Breathe over my garden,*
> *Prays the bride to the north and south winds*
> *To spread its sweet smell around.*
> *Let my beloved come into his garden,*
> *Let him taste its rarest fruits. (4.16)*

Early rabbis included this unlikely book in the Old Testament through interpreting it as an allegory between Jahweh as the lover and the people of Israel as his bride. However, recent scholarship considers that these verses have their origins in an ancient Sumerian cult, whose central rite was a sacred marriage ceremony between King Dumuzi and Inanna, the goddess of life and fertility.[22] The Song of Songs became very popular in the 12th century, when Bernard of Clairvaux formulated the doctrine of Mary's immaculate conception, hence the 'sealed fountain' was taken as referring to her chastity and purity. Bernard was passionately devoted to Mary and composed prayers like troubadour love-songs, which raised her cult to new heights in the Age of Chivalry. He gave the Song of Songs a central place in his sermons. The words of the bride:

> *I am the Rose of Sharon,*
> *The lily of the valleys* [23]

have long been associated with Mary, although in the earliest commentaries, the bride is said to be the Church.[24]

Here Mary becomes more than the passive womb, the *Theotokos,* or 'God-Bearer'. She is also the lover, wooed by Christ, who longs for her to unlock her garden to himself, the bridegroom. This bears a marked resemblance to the mystery religions of the Great Mother in which the Lady is the mother and bride of her own son, who may be depicted both as the infant she suckles and as a young king enthroned beside her. The enclosed garden is also the seat of the individual soul, so the poem can be read as an allegory of the union of the soul with its divine spouse, imagery that was later taken up by the alchemists to symbolise the *coniunctio,* or mystic union of the opposites, as we shall see later.

Some medieval paintings portray Mary crowned with a rose coronet or holding a white rose. Here she has become Queen of Heaven within a celestial Garden of Paradise, a place beyond time and space, a sanctuary of mystery and wisdom. Eithne Wilkins, in her remarkable work on the rosary, *The Rose-Garden Game,* describes her as:

> *...the perfected soul, that is, the soul of the initiate, the one who has 'attained the rose', the personification of the aspiring, the ascending principle in human beings. She is of such perfection that the Wisdom can breathe within her and unite with her. She is the matrix in which human nature becomes perfect and as the human being assumed into heaven to be its queen she embodies the apotheosis towards which all strive.[25]*

The rose takes the place of a sceptre, suggesting that her queenly power comes from divine love rather than worldly authority. Love is the only key that can unlock the door to the *hortus conclusus* and reveal the secret of the hidden rose.

Mary's garden is surrounded by a trellis of red and white roses on a glowing golden ground. Their blossoms are also scattered among other plants, and some are being gathered by angels, who flutter around her like brightly feathered birds. Behind her is 'the sealed fountain', another title of the Virgin, which corresponds to the Fountain of Life in Eden. Her gaze is inward and inscrutable, as she sits with one hand supporting the Child, while the other points towards her heart. The golden-haired infant looks intently down at a holy book read by four angels. A peacock, symbol of immortality, perches gracefully on the trellis. In the foreground sits Saint Catherine of Alexandria with her iconic wheel and sword. She is weaving a garland of roses, helped by an angel, perhaps to be the wedding crown at her mystic marriage to Christ, as the legend relates. Her presence reminds us that it is within the rose garden that the soul unites with God.

Madonna of the Rose Garden by Stefano da Zevio,
Italy, 15th century

The Basket of Roses

Other Christian holy women have their own rose legends.
Saint Dorothea, a 4th century Christian living in
Caesarea, refused to give up her faith and was condemned to
death by decapitation. On the way to her execution, a 'scribe
of the realm' named Theophilus sneeringly asked her to
bring him roses and apples from the 'Paradise' she claimed
she was going to. Suddenly a mysterious child appeared
before her bearing a basket of three roses and three apples.
Dorothea asked him to take the basket to Theophilus. The
year after she was martyred, the little Christ child brought
the apples and roses to Theophilus in the dead of winter,
which inspired him to convert to Christianity. Dorothea is
the patron saint of gardeners.

The rose garden motif also gave rise to 'devotional garden allegories' – books of religious stories produced in Germany and the Netherlands between the 13th and 16th centuries. Drawing heavily upon the imagery of the Song of Songs, they describe the soul's communion with her divine Beloved, and the spiritual delights that await her in the garden. The garden itself represents the heart or perhaps, outwardly, the cloistered life, and the plants cultivated there are qualities that are pleasing to the divine spouse. In a few stories the garden is furnished with a bridal bed strewn with flowers, music – and even wine. Here the bride may sit weaving a garland of roses for her Beloved as she dreams of the mystical union that is to come. [26]

To the modern mind these tales read more like the erotic songs of courtly love rather than virtuous fare for pious Christians. One of these, *Our Lady Mary's Rose Garden*, written by two 15th century Carthusian monks, tells a story in which the Son of the Most High seeks a 'lovely, tender, fragrant rose' to take her back to his father's kingdom 'as a king's son does a beloved bride.'[27] In another, Christ's union with Mary leads to her being crowned as Queen of Heaven and Eden is restored to humankind:

For when this beautiful rose, Mary, began to bloom, the winter of our sadness passed away, the summer of eternal joy began to arrive, and the May of eternal delight to shine. And with her was given back to us the greening, delightful paradise. (lines 205-6) [28]

These lines carry an unmistakable echo of classical goddesses like Aphrodite who personify the renewal of the land at the coming of Spring.

The monks also developed a special kind of prayer-book, or psalter, called a rosary, a word that could either refer to a rose garland or rose garden. To recite a series of prayers addressed to Mary was seen as weaving a chaplet of roses, grown in the garden of the heart, to present to her as a gift.

Rosaries were also designed in picture form only, depicting scenes from the life of Christ and Mary for the mainly illiterate populace. A written or pictorial rosary served as an instructional manual and mnemonic device to help the worshipper keep track of the meditations performed using prayer beads. This eventually led to the beads themselves being called rosaries.

To most of us today, a rosary conjures up a picture of the circle of beads on a string used to keep count of devotional prayers. Its origin is pre-Christian, dating back at least as far as ancient India, where it is mentioned in the Bhagavad Gita. Known as a *mala*, meaning 'garland', the string represents the universal spirit on which all of creation is threaded. The sacred sound known as a *mantra* is repeatedly chanted for every bead counted, a practice designed to induce a higher state of consciousness. Prayer beads are still used today by Hindus and Buddhists, and having spread westward to the Arab world, are also part of Islamic worship. In the 3rd century, Christian hermits, Paul of Thebes and St Anthony, used a similar system of knotted string and pebbles to keep track of the prayers that they recited ceaselessly throughout the day.

In Europe, Catholic prayer beads were originally associated with Mary and her rose. A rosary was usually made from glass or wooden beads, or carved from precious stones for the rich, and developed as a string of one hundred and fifty small beads and fifteen larger ones, divided into fifteen sets of ten small and one large bead. The word 'bead' is derived from the old English *bede,* prayer. In the original design, somewhat modified in recent years, the first large bead is for the *Pater Noster,* (the Lord's Prayer), the smaller ones for the *Ave Maria,* recited ten times, and the next largest one for the *Gloria.* Each set is dedicated

The exquisite rosary of Catherine of Cleves encircles a miniature depiction of the *Adoration of the Magi,* from the 15th century prayer-book, the *Hours of Catherine of Cleves.*

to a meditation on one of the fifteen divine mysteries in the lives of Mary and Christ, and the worshipper reflects on these and contemplates their significance for his or her own life. The practice is still very much alive and evolving today.

Far from waning when the Marian cult had its day, the rosary continued to be a precious icon for the worshipper, especially in times of deadly disasters such as the Black Plague, providing a small measure of comfort – something to hold onto in times of trouble, especially in the final hours. It also became invaluable after the Protestant Reformation in England, when Roman Catholic worship was punishable by death. Praying the rosary was one of the few ways in which the devout could practice their religion, since something so small could be easily hidden from view in a pocket or sewn into a lady's dress.[29] The rosary is still an alive and evolving part of Catholic worship today, for these small, portable circlets of beads have developed into a simple, yet sophisticated technology, packed with a density of meaning for which no literacy is required. As each bead is moved along the thread, the supplicant becomes a pilgrim crossing a chain-link bridge, trusting that the Mother, the 'source of all saving grace', the one who is closest to God, is waiting in welcome on the other side.

DANTE'S CELESTIAL ROSE

The masterwork of Italy's greatest poet, Dante Alighieri (1265-1321), is the epic poem, La Divina Commedia (The Divine Comedy), an allegory of the soul's progress towards God. There is evidence to suggest that Dante was an initiate and leader within the Knights Templar

The Celestial Rose, Dante's Vision of Heaven,
from a 15th century manuscript.

and that the series of 'heavens' described in the *Paradiso*
referred to ascending degrees of initiation in the order.
The model of three worlds and a descent into infernal
regions followed by an ascent to celestial realms is a
feature of many ancient esoteric traditions.[30] It may be

that this was the context in which Dante attained his famous mystic vision of a celestial rose.

The poem unfolds over three canticles, beginning with the *Inferno*, where Dante descends into the depths of Hell and encounters the souls of the damned. In the second canticle, *Purgatorio,* he climbs out of the abyss to ascend the mountain of Purgatory. In the third and final canticle, *Paradiso*, he ascends through the planetary spheres of the Ptolemaic universe to the highest heaven, the Empyrean, where, guided by his beloved Beatrice, he has an ecstatic vision of a huge, glorious Rose formed from a ray of reflected heavenly light. The souls of the blessed are enthroned upon each of its petals, which emerge from the centre of the flower in concentric circles, like the thousand-petalled lotus in the sacred art of India. This Celestial Rose is white, a symbol of Divine Love and heavenly perfection, in contrast with the red rose of earthly love. Its golden centre reflects the light of God's glory, and from it rises the fragrance of praise like incense. Above the Rose, the light of God blazes forth like the sun, shining down beams of heavenly radiance to all those below. Hosts of angels, with golden wings and faces like living flame, fly between God and the celestial rose like a swarm of bees, bringing the nectar of Divine Love to the blessed ones.

Beatrice leaves Dante to take her place on one of the petals, and a new guide appears in the shape of a gentle old man, who turns out to be Saint Bernard of Clairvaux. He draws Dante's attention to the top of the Rose where there is a brilliant flame surrounded by thousands of angels, singing. In the centre of the flame is Mary, enthroned as Queen of Heaven, whose sight renders Dante speechless with joy. She is the epitome of pure love, compassion and heavenly grace. Bernard prays to her that through her intercession, Dante may experience the full glory of God, and exhorts all the blessed souls, especially Beatrice, to add their power to his plea. The prayer is granted: Dante looks into the infinite glory of the Light Divine and beholds the unity of all creation, a triple rainbow of light representing the Trinity, and the figure of Christ unified with the eternal being of the Godhead. All is bound together with the 'Love that moves the sun and the other stars'.

The Rose Window

*When the magnificent Gothic cathedrals soared above the
skyline of medieval cities in the 12th and 13th centuries,
many of them displayed 'rose windows', beautiful circular
mandalas illuminated with richly coloured stained glass.
Their shape bears little resemblance to a botanical rose
yet serves as a reminder of one of the supposed origins
of its name: rota, a wheel. The sun that streams through
to dazzle the dark interior with an unearthly radiance
symbolises the Divine Light of God refracted into the
glorious colours of creation. When Dante chose a celestial
white rose to be the ultimate symbol of his Paradise, he
may have been thinking of windows such as these. Abbot
Suger of the great Abbey Saint-Denis near Paris, said
that rose windows were able to*

*transform that which is material to that which is immaterial...
Then it seems to me that I see myself dwelling, as it were, in
some strange region of the universe which neither exists entirely
in the slime of the earth nor entirely in the purity of Heaven;
and that, by the grace of God, I can be transported from this
inferior to that higher world.[31]*

*Many Gothic cathedrals were built over centres of
pilgrimage in pre-Christian times. In France a number
of these have been identified as places of goddess worship.
With Bernard of Clairvaux's promotion of the Holy
Virgin cult, some of the finest churches and cathedrals of
this period were dedicated to Notre-Dame – Our Lady.
So it is that Mary, usually portrayed with the divine
Child, can often be discovered in the centre of these
'roses of light'.*

The North Window of Chartres Cathedral

Perhaps the most famous of these graces the cathedral of Our Lady of Chartres in northern France. It was built on one of the most important holy sanctuaries of the Celtic tribes in ancient Gaul, dedicated to a virgin goddess about to give birth to a miraculous child. This magnificent building was constructed according to the principles of sacred geometry as a way to align this sacred space with the harmony and order of the cosmos. There are three magnificent rose windows in the cathedral. Christ appears as the central figure in the west and south windows, with Mary in the centre of the north window, commonly known as the Rose de France.

The daylight that blazes through the brilliant red hues of the south window creates a striking contrast to the softly glowing blues of the one in the North, suggesting the Sun and Moon. Mary is seated with the Christ Child on her lap, holding a sceptre topped with a fleur-de-lis. Doves of the Holy Spirit descend towards her, seraphim and cherubim hover around her, and the kings of Judah, her forefathers, form a circle around her. Titus Burkhardt, in his book on Chartres, writes:

Here the cosmic wheel has become a rose, a flower of purity, innocence, and nobility of soul, whose calyx opens like a wheel, to receive within itself the sun of the Holy Spirit.[32]

Among the Jewish populations of Europe, the 12th and 13th centuries were a time of spiritual renewal. The Jewish rabbis and scholars of Southern France and Northern Spain composed seminal books on the Kabbalah, the main body of Jewish mystical writings. This system of esoteric teachings is designed to explain the relationship between the eternal, infinite Creator and the finite, created universe. Just as the archetype of the sacred feminine returned to religious life in the Christian world, the medieval kabbalists began to talk about the feminine face of God. This is the Shekinah, whose name means *the indwelling*, referring to the immanent presence of God, or the Divine within ourselves and all of creation. She has been called the focus of the 'divine and human search for wholeness', the 'bride of God within God, mother of the world and feminine side of the divine'.[33] The first lines of the Zohar, or Book of Brilliance, written at the end of the 13th century in Spain, describe the Shekinah as a rose among thorns, the purity of divine beauty that emerges out of evil. She has two aspects: an 'upper rose' that dwells in the pure world of spirit, and a 'lower rose', the presence of the Divine that dwells within material creation. The lower rose is outwardly identified with the community of Israel and inwardly with the individual soul. The rose of the Shekinah has thirteen petals which correspond to her thirteen measures of mercy. The five sepals that hold the petals are compared to the five fingers that raise the cup of wine in blessing, which transforms it into a Cup of Salvation, filled with the Light of God

Mother Rose

The pagan rose goddess was not entirely forgotten in the Middle Ages. In southern Germany, the goddess Hulda was also known as Mutter Rose and Frau Rose. She lived in a magical cave in the mountains of Thuringia called the Venusberg. It was also known as the Rose Garden or Rose Grove and the witches who worshipped her there were called 'Visitors of the Grove'. A story from the 13th century tells how Tannhäuser, a minnesinger, or troubadour, ventured into the Mountain of Venus, despite being warned that it was the home of a terrible demon. He followed a passage which led him to a vast chamber filled with glistening stalactites.

A soft voice called his name, and out of the shadows came a beautiful woman dressed in flowing silver robes and wearing a garland of roses in her shining hair. Tannhäuser recognized her as Mother Rose, the pagan goddess who had been denounced by the church as a demon.

He fell in love with her, and they lived happily together for a year, until Tannhäuser began to think of the world he had left behind and of the teachings of the church he had followed faithfully all his life. He travelled to Rome seeking forgiveness from the Pope, but His Holiness refused, saying there could be no mercy for one who had consorted with a demon. Holding up his papal staff, the Pope swore that forgiveness was no more possible than his staff blooming again. In great sorrow, Tannhäuser left for the mountains and was never seen again. He had returned to Mother Rose, who had shown him only love and compassion. Three days later the Pope's staff burst into blossom. Realising that this was a divine message, he sent for Tannhäuser, but though sought far and wide, he was never found.

A medieval garden in *Le Roman de la Rose*

The Romance of the Rose

One of the greatest works of medieval literature is The Romance of the Rose, an allegory of courtly love composed by two French poets in the 13th century. It tells of a young man who dreams of a beautiful four-square garden, Love's Paradise. Here he is captivated by the sight of a rosebud, which becomes a symbol of his beloved. He has to go through severe trials before he finally reaches his Rose with the help of Venus herself. Although conventionally viewed as a work extolling the art of sensual love, some theorists have declared it to be an erudite philosophical work, a Christian allegory, an alchemical treatise, or a coded description of spiritual initiation, whose true purpose was deliberately concealed in allegorical imagery to avoid the censure of the church.

The 20th century esoteric scholar, A. E. Waite, writes:

The 'Romance of the Rose' is the epic of ancient France. It is a profound work in a trivial guise, as learned an exposition of the mysteries of occultism as that of Apuleius.[34]

MEDITATION II –
CHAPEL OF THE ROSE GRAIL

Close your eyes and take some long, slow, deep breaths, letting go of all outer concerns. Let your consciousness sink down and down into silence...

It is twilight and you are walking through a dim brown forest in winter. The trees are bare and there is no sound of birdsong. All the animals are in their winter sleep and a deep silence pervades the land. Even your footsteps on the brown damp earth of the path make no noise.

The trees thin out, and the path leads into a glade in the very heart of the woods in which stands the Chapel in the Old Forest, a simple foursquare building made of blocks of old grey stone, covered by a patchwork of lichens and moss. In a rounded archway is set a sturdy oaken door. You walk up to the door, and clasp the round iron ring, which is icy cold to the touch. You turn it, and the door slowly creaks open. You walk over the threshold, closing the door behind you. A heavy curtain of burgundy velvet covers the door on the inside, and you gently push this aside and find yourself standing on the stone flags of the chapel.

The chapel walls are set with four great, arched windows to the four directions, something which was not apparent from outside. Before you to the East is a window of glowing gold and amber stained glass depicting the Archangel Raphael. On your right, to the South, is a window of scarlet, orange and ruby through which the sun shines, dappling the stone floor with splashes of fiery colour. Here is depicted the Archangel Michael. On your left to the North is a soft green window with emerald lights, depicting the Archangel Auriel. You take a few steps into the chapel, turn around, and gaze up above the door through which you entered at a glowing blue circular window depicting the Archangel Gabriel. Turning around again, you see that the Chapel is simply furnished, with a bare stone altar in the centre, an ancient edifice that looks like it was carved from a single rock. It is bare of all ornament except for one white pillar candle. As you gaze at your surroundings, a small door on the far side of the altar in the northeast corner opens quietly and a figure stands there – a slight man with a white beard and a chaplet of oak leaves about his head. It is the Hermit of the Chapel, and even though he is half-concealed in the shadows, you sense a kindly and welcoming presence. Silently, he motions you to the stone altar.

As you gaze at the altar, a line of liquid fire licks across its surface and the shape of a Grail emerges upon it: a simple long-stemmed chalice of pale gold. It seems to have emerged out of the stone itself, and now stands revealed, shimmering in its own soft luminescence. A column of pure white light streams down from above and fills the Grail to the brim. The light overflows and pours down over the stone altar, illuminating carvings of plants, animals and figures that you had not noticed before. The light has made the altar a Living Rock. Now from the four windows of the Archangels, you see two beams of light crossing from South to North and from East to West, forming an equal armed cross intersecting just above the Grail. At its centre, a shimmering Rose appears out of the heart of the light, iridescent with every colour like a glowing jewel. The exquisite beauty of this living Rose of Light fills the chapel with an indescribably beautiful fragrance, illuminating everything around, glowing out of heart of light. You now become aware that you are not alone, that many other souls are with you around the altar. There may be some here you recognise...

The Rose glows and grows until it fills the whole place and the Chapel disappears... and now you see that each soul gathered around has become one of its many petals, as you have, too... Together all have become the Rosa Mundi, the Rose of the

World. Some petals are wider open than others... All are slowly opening so that in time the heart of the Rose will be revealed to all. Feel yourself as one of the myriad petals... Breathe in and out the scent of the Rose... and gaze upon the golden heart within its centre...

Then gradually you become aware of a high ethereal melody, faint at first, then growing into audible sound from high above you, like a heavenly choir of voices. Gazing upwards, you are aware of angelic figures of iridescent hues hovering and drifting above you in the empyrean. The notes of their song become visible, shimmering essences of Light, that drop gently onto each of the petals of the Rose, so that each of the upturned petals of souls receive the blessing of this divine alchemical dew, which is pure Love and pure Light, given freely to all... *(Pause for a long time to receive this heavenly gift.)*

When you are ready to return, allow the light to fade... See the Rose merge back into the Grail and the altar. All the images, including the circle of souls, fade away, in the now dim and silent Chapel. . . At this point you may sense an invitation from the Hermit to sit and speak with him in a quiet place, for he is a wise guide, an Anamcara, or Soul-friend. You may have questions about what you have witnessed or ask him for spiritual direction...

When you are ready to leave the Chapel, the Hermit gives you a blessing and accompanies you to the door. As you step outside, you may be surprised to see that the wintry trees are now touched with young green buds of Spring, which rustle in a gentle breeze as you make your way back.

Now with each breath become aware of your physical body... It is time to return, bringing with you the remembrance of all that has passed.

Write down your experience in your journal.

CHAPTER THREE

THE SCENT OF PARADISE

What was said to the rose that made it open
was said to me here in my heart.
– Rumi

he Rose was not only the definitive symbol of the sacred in medieval Europe; it also blossomed in the gardens – and in the psyche – of those living further east. The first Persian gardens were designed to represent the beauty and harmony of the primordial paradise, an idea which may have its origins as far back as the Sumerian period in Mesopotamia. Paradise literally means a walled garden, from the Persian *pairidaeza*: *pairi* meaning 'around' and *daeza* meaning 'wall'. The walled garden provided much needed elements of water and shade in the harsh desert landscape of the Middle East. Designed to be nurturing, to offer refuge and respite from the oppressive heat, arid soil and gritty winds, it was a secret oasis for body and soul.

A 16th century Persian miniature depicts the Mughal Emperor
Babur supervising the layout of a fourfold garden.

The four walls were divided into equal parts by channels of water in the shape of a cross, to reflect the division of the universe into four directions, four seasons, and the four elements: water, wind, soil and fire, according to the cosmology of Zoroastrianism, the pre-Islamic religion of Persia. The garden became an earthly reflection of the spiritual world, a universal symbol of cosmic order and harmony.

The walls were made of thick solid bricks, to give a sense of seclusion. Ponds and pools supplied the water for verdant trees and luxuriant plants, divided by a network of symmetrical pathways along which to walk and wander. The sacred centre might be marked by a fountain or flowering tree, both symbols of the creative source of life that emerges mysteriously from hidden depths and inexhaustibly renews itself. In the larger, royal gardens there might be a pavilion overlooking a large central pool, the main source of irrigation, which represented the cosmic ocean.

The importance of the rose in the paradise garden is indicated in a passage from the *Avesta*, the Zoroastrian sacred texts, where it is called 'a messenger of the garden of souls'. In Islamic culture, which arrived in the 7th century CE, the fourfold geometry of the walled garden reflected the image of the heavenly Paradise promised by the Qu'ran, with its 'spreading shade', 'fountains of gushing water', and four sacred rivers. Traditional Islamic buildings, whether secular or religious, were built around a courtyard containing a miniature paradise garden and spread throughout the Islamic world from Moorish Spain and North Africa to the India of the Mughals. They can still be seen today in many parts of the Middle East. Emma Clark in her book, *The Art of the Islamic Garden*, describes the purpose of this sanctuary:

> *The garden was for resting and taking refuge in, and for delighting in the cooling and soothing properties of water; for the aesthetic and sensory delights of flowers, the scent of blossom, the song of the birds, as well as the protective shade of trees. All these things were enjoyed, not for their sake alone, but in the full knowledge that they were a reflection of the bliss of the heavenly gardens to come.* [35]

Since Paradise is in essence a hidden and secret dimension that dwells in the innermost soul, the garden was known as *al-jannah* meaning 'concealment', similar to the *hortus conclusus* of the mediaeval monastic garden. The Qur'an speaks of the 'Garden of the Soul and Garden of the Heart', reserved for the devout disciple, and a 'Garden of the Spirit and Garden of the Essence' reserved for those closest to God. They are sometimes referred to as 'gardens underneath which rivers flow', a metaphor for the ever-flowing waters of the spirit which cleanse, purify and refresh the soul. In these gardens, the only word ever spoken is 'Peace' and the gardener is Allah.

The petals of the flower on the right spell the '99 Most Beautiful Names of God' (Asma ul Husna); on the left, the '99 Noble Names of the Prophet Muhammad' (Asma un Nabi). The central rose contains descriptions of the Holy Prophet, while the rosebuds around the lower section are the names of the family and companions.

The Rose of Muhammad from the manuscript,
Akhlaq i Rasul Allah, Turkey 1708.

FLOWER OF HEAVEN

There were two types of Islamic garden: the *bostan*, or
orchard, that provided trees for fruit and shade, and
the *gulistan*, or flower garden, prized for its beauty and
fragrance. Such was the importance of the rose that the
word *gul* means both 'flower' and 'rose'. It was known as
the flower of heaven, an embodiment of divine beauty,
and also symbolised the Prophet Muhammad himself, as
the chief bloom in Allah's garden. Its exquisite fragrance
has always played an important part in Islamic traditions.
As part of the annual Muslim pilgrimage to Mecca, rose

water is sprinkled over the black cloth covering the Ka'aba stone, and rose oil is burnt in the surrounding lamps. Not surprisingly, it became the most important symbol in the poetry of the Sufis. Sufism is the mystical branch of Islam, said to have its roots in an older mystical tradition that emphasised the essential unity of religions and the centrality of love. The Sufi teacher, Suhrawardi of Aleppo, had a teaching method called the Path of the Rose which some have seen as a precursor to Rosicrucianism.[36] The Qadiri Sufi order, founded in the 12th century by Abdul-Qadir Gilani, was known as The Rose of Baghdad, and his order's symbol is the rose. Qadiri dervishes dance wearing a rose of green and white cloth, with a six-pointed star in the middle.

SEEKING THE BELOVED

In the Sufi tradition, the rose garden was the inner sanctuary that can be found within the heart. In this vein, the 15th century poet, Kabir, exhorted his readers:

> *Do not go into the garden of flowers!*
> *Oh friend, go not there;*
> *In your body is the garden of flowers.*

Sufi poems from Persia and Turkey bear titles such as *Rosebed, Rose Garden, Rose-parterre.* The most famous of these is the *Gulshan-i raz,* The Rose Garden of Mystery, sometimes translated as *The Secret Rose Garden.* Composed by the 13th century poet, Sa'd ud Din Mahmud Shabistari, it is considered to be one of the greatest works of Persian Sufism.

The renowned 13th century Persian poet, Sa'di of Shiraz, was walking in a garden with a friend who began gathering flowers. Sa'di contemplated their ephemeral nature and was inspired to write his famous book, *Gulistan* (Rose Garden), to express eternal truths that would not die.

In the Paradise garden within, the rose is both the unfolding human soul and the Divine Beloved which she seeks. In the words of the renowned scholar of Islam, Annemarie Schimmel:

> *The true lover who has experienced this blossoming of the eternal Rose in himself understands that the gardens of this world are only a lovely pretext for the Beloved to veil and unveil Himself at the same time...*[37]

The 20th century Sufi teacher, Hazrat Inayat Khan, describes the spiritual development of the soul as an opening rose:

> *Just as the rose consists of many petals held together, so the person who attains to the unfoldment of the soul begins to show many different qualities. The qualities emit fragrance in the form of a spiritual personality. The rose has a beautiful structure, and the personality which proves the unfoldment of the soul has also a fine structure, in manner, in dealing with others, in speech, in action. The atmosphere of a spiritual being pervades the air like the perfume of a rose.[38]*

Like Dante's image of the Celestial Rose, the rose is viewed as a symbol for the Oneness which underlies all forms, while the petals represent the multiplicity of its expression in the physical world:

> *In the state of union the single beings of the world are one,*
> *All the petals of the rose are together one. [39]*

The many difficulties and setbacks encountered on the spiritual path are represented by its thorns. These are the weapons of the ego that engender the sharp pain of separation, frustrating the Divine Lover in her search for union with the Beloved.

> *Before a flower can open in the rose garden*
> *thousands of thorns come to pierce it.[40]*

Yet they play their part in deterring the profane and the faint-hearted, emphasising the arduous nature of a spiritual journey that is never to be undertaken lightly.

On a deeper level it is often the thorns of life that pierce the heart open so that, in desperation, it seeks beyond the unreliable world of human relationships for lasting fulfilment in the true Source of Love. In the ecstasy of that experience, all our human hurts and heartbreaks dwindle into insignificance:

> *Gaze in wonder at the infinite rose garden,*
> *don't consider that thorn that wounded your foot.* [41]

Yet ultimately, thorn and blossom are two inseparable aspects of one plant, just as the individual is not ultimately separate from the Absolute, which is why Rumi said, 'A rose's rarest essence lives in the thorn'.

ENTERING THE ROSE GARDEN

The verses of Jalaluddin Rumi, the greatest of all the mystical Sufi poets, explore the soul's passage through the rose-garden as a journey from innocence to experience. To do otherwise is to live in a state of dullness and contraction. Rumi captures the feeling of exhilaration that often accompanies the first stages of the spiritual path:

> *Each moment from all sides rushes to us the call of love.*
> *We are running to contemplate its vast green field.*
> *Do you want to come with us?*
> *This is not the time to stay at home,*
> *but to go out and give yourself to the rose garden.*

The dawn of joy has arisen,
and this is the moment of vision.[42]

To enter the Rose Garden is to say yes to Love's invitation to be wholly open and undefended, daring to be fully alive to its beauty and ecstasy.

Unlike the Garden of Eden, the primordial paradise of 'Adam and maiden', this garden is not for the innocent or untried soul, for it makes us utterly vulnerable and unprotected against its requirement for the whole-hearted submission of the self. It soon becomes clear that the willingness to offer oneself up completely incurs the risk of losing everything one formerly held dear, especially the apparently separate self. When we are 'cooked' in Love's crucible, the false identity is discovered to be an illusion. When it withers and dies it is transformed into a fertile compost for the true Self to emerge:

Where would the full Rose grow
but in rich dark dirt?
How but through love's agony
could you become love's timeless bliss? [43]

Only by shedding every defence in the ego's armoury will we be allowed into the secret sanctuary within the rose garden, a place of impossible beauty that the soul may enter only after a lifetime of untold losses and betrayals in the wilderness of the world:

Love drives you mad
from revelation to revelation

through ordeal after ordeal
until humble and broken
you are carried tenderly
into the heart of the rose.[44]

Beyond innocence and experience lies a place of timeless peace and joy that can only be discovered beyond the world of opposites, residing within the boundless true Self. This, Rumi calls 'the rose garden that is neither outside this world nor within it . . . A garden neither autumn or winter makes afraid'.[45] In his book, 'Table-talk', he offers a breathtaking vision of what – and Who – awaits us there:

When Grace wills, you will know this world to be the Rose Garden of rose gardens, a paradise where nothing is ever born and nothing ever dies. You will realise that you and its Gardener are one heart, one breath. This is the heaven the Beloved keeps for the lovers; no one arrives in it who has not been through ring after ring of fire.[46]

The Nightingale and the Rose

In Persian legend, the rose was originally white. The nightingale was so in love with her beauty that he spent every night pouring out his love in ecstatic song. But in his longing to be united with her, he flew too close, and a thorn pierced his breast. The blood stained the petals crimson and ever after the rose became red. In Sufi poetry, the nightingale is regarded as the soul's yearning for union with the Divine Beloved. The Turkish poet Yunus Emre eloquently summarises this:

A nightingale falls in love with the Rose.
The whole love affair begins
with just one look from God.[47]

It is the nightingale's suffering that makes his song all the more exquisite, just as the most beautiful poetry arises from the unbearable pain of separation in the soul of the mystic in search of God. Rumi however knew that, ultimately, separation is an illusion:

The nightingale of those whom He grants a mystical rapture
has its own rose garden in itself. [48]

Deep within our own soul is found that which we seek outside and is the object of our deepest longing – to be one with the Rose.

MEDITATION III –
THE ROSE GARDEN

Close your eyes and take some long, slow, deep breaths, letting go of all outer concerns. Let your consciousness sink down and down into silence...

You find yourself trudging through an endless barren desert. The only sound is the eerie whistling of the wind as it sweeps over the sand, shaping it into strange mounds and gullies. No birds or other creatures are apparent, but occasionally you can see the tracks of lizards and scorpions criss-crossing the dunes. The sun beats down over this harsh and desolate wilderness, and soon you feel scorched by its merciless heat, and dry as dust from the wind that stings you with razor-like shards of sand. Your throat is parched, and your weary footsteps are beginning to falter...

But at last, lifting your smarting eyes to the horizon, you begin to see something take shape, shimmering like a mirage in the heat haze. As you draw closer, you see it is a wall made of thick, even bricks, in the centre of which is a small door. You can hear the sound of running water within, and your heart leaps within you. You knock on the door and after a pause, are aware of quiet footsteps approaching.

A voice speaks, asking you why you have made this long journey through the desert to the Rose Garden.

You reply that you have come to meet the Beloved.

The door opens, but you do not see who opened it. Although this is puzzling, as soon as you step inside, your attention is immediately drawn towards the beautiful garden within. Cypress trees offer welcome shade, while others hang heavy with ripe golden apricots and peaches. The scent of roses fills the air, which here is cool and fresh. Four straight paths lead from the four directions to the centre where there is a clear, round pool. On the far side, the water flows into a channel and thence into many streams to irrigate the garden.

After moistening your parched throat from one of these, you find yourself walking down one of the paths, drawn towards the still, shining pool. It is surrounded by rose bushes; it is their heavenly fragrance that fills the whole garden. Every now and then a few petals drift down onto its surface, and glide away down the channel.

Then a nightingale breaks forth into liquid song, and as if in response to its call of Love, your heart is filled with an almost unbearable, deep yearning for the One for whom you have journeyed so far. And then – in the mirror-like surface of the pool, appears the reflection of someone standing behind you. The One you have come to meet is here. Turn around and let whatever happens next be between you and this Being of Love...

When the time comes for you to leave the Rose Garden, the Beloved touches your heart, leaving an indelible imprint of their presence, a signature of Love that will always be with you, wherever you are: a key to help you return to this place again and again...

Then become aware with each breath that you are back in your physical body and in your room. When you are ready, open your eyes. After a while, write down your experience and any thoughts in your journal.

CHAPTER FOUR

THE ALCHEMICAL ROSE

he Rose plays a central role in the ancient art and science of alchemy. Alchemists wrote about their work using a special language of symbol, metaphor, and allegory, 'so that they can only be understood by saints, sages, and souls endowed with understanding.'[49] Many alchemical illustrations take the form of extremely complex and beautiful emblems which have been compared to the yantras and mandalas of Eastern religions – symbols for spiritual contemplation and meditation that in themselves have the power to alter consciousness. Different substances and processes are portrayed as elements of the living world, including birds, animals, mythical beasts like gryphons and dragons, heavenly bodies, trees and plants. The rose is one of alchemy's fundamental symbols: the 16th century alchemists called the rose *flos sapientium,* the 'flower of the Wise'. The 17th century alchemist and physician, Count Michael Maier, described the rose as 'the first, most beautiful and perfect of all flowers', and went on to say,

'… even as the natural Rose is a pleasure to the senses and life of man, on account of its sweetness and salubrity, so is the Philosophical Rose exhilarating to the heart and giver of strength to the brain.'[50]

Alchemy originated in Hellenized Egypt in the first few centuries BCE. The origin of its name is a mystery: It may come from the Arabic *al-kimiya*, from the Greek *chymeia,* the art of pouring molten metal, or from *keme,* black, referring to the fertile black earth that bordered the Nile. The knowledge and practice of alchemy spread through Europe in the 12th century due to Greek and Arab

Alchemical emblem XLII in Michael Maier's *Atalanta Fugiens*, 1618

Let Nature be your guide, and with your Art,
Follow keenly her lead, without which you go astray.
With sapiens as staff, seasoned experience vivifies sight.
Let Learning be your lamp, dispelling dark.

influences and became very popular in the Middle Ages. It also enjoyed a resurgence in the 16th and 17th centuries among the Rosicrucians who viewed it as an integral part of the Hermetic teachings. One of the first and most famous of the Rosicrucian alchemical texts was *The Chymical Wedding of Christian Rosenkreuz*, an allegory of the soul's journey to God through the alchemical process of transmutation, as we will see in the next chapter.

THE SOUL OF ALCHEMY

It is popularly believed that the alchemists' chief goal was to transmute base metal into gold, and certainly, there were those who embarked upon it purely for monetary gain. But most alchemists poured scorn on these 'puffers' – so called because they were always stoking up the fire with their bellows – who debased the Royal Art and had no real understanding of its spiritual nature. This was especially the case in the 17th and 18th centuries when alchemy was regarded as an authentic spiritual practice that offered a sevenfold path to initiation.

Alchemy had its origins in the ancient crafts of metallurgy and blacksmithing where the practitioner magically revealed the hidden beauty of the dull ore within the earth and transformed it into objects of shining beauty. Alchemists were influenced by the Gnostic view that most metals, like the Earth plane in general, were imperfect, yet they could be developed and brought to perfection in the laboratory. The task was to bring about the metamorphosis of the six 'lower' metals – lead, iron, tin, mercury, copper and silver – and turn them into gold, the seventh, most perfect and incorruptible of all substances. Through following the wisdom of the 'Book of Nature' and the divine spark within, the physical world can be perfected.

For transmutations that occurred in the laboratory also had to take place within the soul of the alchemist. The work of changing lead into gold was not just viewed as an outer process involving metals but was at the same time a spiritual process designed to integrate the personality and lead the soul to divine perfection. The seven metals were seen as the earthly counterparts to the seven planets of classical astrology which influence and shape the personality of the earthbound human being. The inner work of the alchemist was to rise above each of these planetary influences in turn so as to 'lead out the gold within' and achieve the radiance and beauty of the illumined and awakened soul. This meant that practical work in the laboratory was accompanied by devotional exercises, prayers to God, and the invocation of angels and other intermediary spirits.

This was the *magnum opus,* or Great Work, of the alchemist, and its transmutation could only be achieved through creating the *lapis philosophorum*, or Philosopher's Stone, a powder or tincture which could transmute imperfect matter into the purity and perfection of gold. The Stone was believed to be an elixir of life, capable of curing all diseases, restoring youth and even bestowing immortality. Yet it is described in mysterious terms as 'a stone, yet not a stone', which can be found everywhere in nature but is despised or ignored. It is unknown and yet known to everyone.

The creation of the Philosopher's Stone begins with the *prima materia,* the 'first material', a mysterious substance which must be acted on by a 'secret fire'. After being moistened with spring dew, it is placed into a hermetically sealed vessel called the Philosophical Egg which is heated slowly over a long period of time. The substance then goes through a threefold process. The first stage is *nigredo,* or blackening, referring to the 'death' of the original substance, in order to remove its impurities. The second stage, when the material is purified and turns white, is called *albedo*, or whitening. At the third and final stage, *rubedo,* or reddening, the material takes on a red tint.[51] The red and white powders signify the creation of the Philosopher's Stone.

Although these colours refer to physically observable changes in the metals within the alchemist's laboratory, they also outline an inner path to spiritual awakening. In fact, there is some likelihood that this and related alchemical processes may be a coded description for Tantric practices, as is the case in Chinese alchemy.[52]

The *prima materia* is the unawakened individual, heavily identified with the egoic self and the body. The first stage, or blackening, comes about when living an ego-centred life is no longer satisfying. There may be a crisis of confidence, traumatic loss, deep depression, or debilitating illness: a 'dark night of the soul'. This passage often occurs at mid-life, as Dante well knew when he wrote his famous line: 'In the middle of the road of my life I awoke in a dark wood where the true way was wholly lost'.

In the next stage, the whitening, we gain an awareness of our deeper identity as a soul. The experience of the

From an emblem by 17th century alchemist, Johann Daniel Mylius. Red and white roses twining around two lit candles speak clearly of alchemy's relationship with the yogic practices which aim to make the kundalini, or serpent energy, rise up two channels on either side of the spine in a spiralling process of awakening.

soul-self is one of being guided by a luminous, gentle light, which, like the moon, purveys a sense of serenity from a higher plane, transforming the stresses of earthly life by showing them to be evanescent and illusory. In Western tradition, the soul is feminine and lunar: often it is at mid-life that living a life based on the personality and its masculine/yang drive for outer achievements is found to be unfulfilling, and there is a yearning for a more feminine/yin, relational, and soul-centred life.

The third stage, the reddening, brings about the dawning consciousness of an even higher reality, in which the soul is experienced as reflecting an even greater Light: the spiritual source which, like the sun in the physical world, is the purveyor of all life. A simple way to grasp this sequence is as a progression from the darkness of night to the whiteness of the moon, the redness of dawn and finally the rising of the golden sun. As the sun warms and gives life to all on earth, so the goal of the alchemist is not just one of personal enlightenment, but of sharing that light and healing warmth with those who still live in the darkness of ignorance and disease.

THE ROSE GARDEN OF THE ALCHEMISTS

Several manuscripts contain the title, 'Rosarium', meaning 'Rose Garden'. This refers to the enclosed and secret garden, the sanctuary, or *temenos,* in which the alchemists did their work to perfect the soul: an imaginal sacred space which was the inner counterpart to the outer, physical laboratory. Here bloomed roses, red and white, representing the tinctures of the Sun and Moon which were brought together in a 'sacred marriage' as part of the alchemical Great Work. The *albedo* stage is symbolised by the white rose, which is associated with the White Queen, the lunar, feminine, passive principle associated with the element mercury. The *rubedo* stage is symbolised by the red rose, associated with the Red King, the solar, masculine, active principle, associated with the chemical sulphur. Within the human experience this refers to the integration of the solar, logical, action-oriented consciousness with the lunar, intuitive, receptive feminine soul. These two separated halves of ourselves must be consciously

King and Queen as Sol and Luna unite in the *coniunctio,* or sacred marriage of the opposites.

conjoined within the human psyche. This is known as the Lesser Work.

On a cosmic level, the sacred marriage symbolises the mystic union of opposites, in which the masculine Spirit, the transcendent principle, is united with the feminine principle of the Earth: a marriage of Spirit and Matter, which brings forth all created life. Only when the soul is integrated fully into our lives can the next stage begin: the transmutation of the integrated self into 'gold' – the radiant spirit which is our divine nature. In alchemical works such as the *Rosarium Philosophorum,* the Rose Garden of the Philosophers, Masculine and Feminine, symbolised by the solar King and lunar Queen, merge as one in the mystical union from which is born the enlightened Self. This is the Greater Work, the hidden treasure within the human heart, often depicted as a golden rose.

The Rose Child

In some texts, the 'chymical wedding' of the Red King and White Queen produces a miraculous child, the filius philosophorum (son of the philosophers). The famous 15th century alchemist, Sir George Ripley, wrote of

the pleasant and dainty Garden of the Philosophers, which beareth the sweet-smelling Roses white and red, abbreviated out of all the Work of the Philosophers, containing in it nothing superfluous or diminished, teaching to make infinitely Gold and Silver.[53]

The alchemical scroll attributed to him shows a Tudor rose with white petals at the centre, contained within red petals. The scroll reads:

Take the fayer Roses, white and red.
And join them well in won bed.
So betw'n these Roses mylde
Thou shalt bring forth a Gloriuse chylde.

From the Ripley Scrowle by Sir George Ripley, 1588, Germany. In spiritual alchemy, the white petals represent the divine consciousness *(Rosa Mystica)* that can be found deep within the red rose of the world *(Rosa Mundi)*.

The Tudor Rose

In the 15th century, a flower with petals of both red and white became an important royal symbol known as the Tudor rose. Although it was created for political reasons, it had its origins in alchemy, which was enjoying a fashion among the nobility of the 15th century. The Tudor rose combines the red rose of Lancaster with the white rose of York. It was designed to herald the unity of the nation now that the Wars of the Roses had been brought to an end with the marriage between Henry VII of Lancaster and Elizabeth of York.

The result of this human alchemical marriage was a flesh-and-blood 'Philosopher's Child', who was named Arthur after the legendary king who had brought peace and unity to Britain. Arthur's birth was arranged to take place at Winchester, the city believed at the time to have been Camelot. An Arthurian Round Table was constructed with a Tudor rose at its centre, to represent, in the words of historian Jonathan Hughes, 'the rose of alchemy, the philosopher's stone, the nation's soul'.[54] It can still be seen today hanging in the Great Hall in Winchester Castle. Sadly, Arthur died at a young age, putting an end to the nation's dreams of a new Golden Age.

The Winchester round table was originally created in the 13th century during the reign of Edward I. It was repainted in the 16th century in the reign of Henry VIII, who acted as the model for King Arthur.

MEDITATION IV –
AN ALCHEMICAL WEDDING

This meditation is based on an allegory of the mystical marriage by German alchemist, Hinricus Madathanus, in 1625. The Stag represents Soul, and the Unicorn, Spirit.

Close your eyes and take some long, slow, deep breaths, letting go of all outer concerns. Let your consciousness sink down and down into silence...

You are walking along a path through a dense forest. You are feeling rather lost because the path winds in and out, and sometimes seems to turn back on itself, and without the sun you have no sense of orientation. As you are starting to wonder how you will find your way out, you see a glimmer of light in the trees, and hear the sound of hooves. You stop short, fearing wild animals, but your fear is soon overcome by amazement: trotting out of the clearing come a golden stag and white unicorn that seem to glow with their own inner light. They bow their heads before you, then turn onto another path, looking back at you once as if encouraging you to follow.

Trusting these magnificent animals, you take this new route, and soon come to the edge of the forest.

You are in a green fertile landscape now, and the stag and unicorn are leading you towards a tall castle with four towers within a circular wall, high up on a hill. When you arrive at the castle gates, they give another bow of their heads, then gallop away back into the forest.

A crowd of people are pouring in through the gates, sweeping you along with them. Soon you find yourself in a courtyard where a wedding is about to take place. The bride is a most beautiful maiden, dressed all in shining white satin, and her groom the most handsome youth, clad all in vivid scarlet. On her head is a silver crown in which is set a jewel like a glowing moon, and she bears a white rose; while he wears a gold crown from which shines forth a lustrous ruby like the sun and carries a red rose. A brilliant star shines down upon them from above.

The young man turns to his bride, saying in a strong voice, 'O Luna, let me be thy husband.' She replies: 'O Sol, I must submit to thee.' At this point there is a loud cheer from the circle of wedding guests, and suddenly a white dove flies down as if out of the star itself, bearing a scroll which reads, 'It is the Spirit which vivifies.'

The bride and groom exchange roses, and hand in hand, walk towards a hexagonal bath in the middle of the courtyard, where they proceed to take off all their clothes and step into the purifying waters within. They embrace passionately, becoming as one being in their ardour, then to your astonishment, they dissolve away completely in the water. Now another figure emerges from the bath in their place: the fruit of their union, a beautiful Golden Child, smiling and laughing with joy.

You sense the presence of one behind you, and turning, you see a woman of late middle age. She is sturdily built and carries an air of authority and wisdom. She wears a white robe covered with a red cloak. This is Maria Prophetissa, the famous alchemist of Alexandria. She speaks:

'Welcome to the Castle of Alchemy where above and below are as One. When the red fire of the sun and the white fire of the moon unite, earth shall become a reflection of the heavens. From the sacred marriage of Soul and Spirit is born the Child that shall unite Heaven and Earth.

For as it was given to me to understand, one becomes two, two becomes three, and out of the third comes the one as the fourth. Which is to say, when we are born there is no separation between us and the world, but then we become individuals, and the world becomes me/you, black/white, male/female. But if we listen to the call of our soul who longs to unite with Spirit again, we give birth to a new Self, a Child of Light who will transform the world.'

You ponder on these words and ask Maria Prophetissa how you may achieve this. What is the first step you must take? In answer, she leads you out of the courtyard and into the castle, leaving the crowds and the noise of celebration behind. Pointing to a spiral stone staircase winding up into a tower, she tells you there are seven levels to climb before you can reach a place of transformation. You must start down here in a secret chamber – and strangely enough, she tells you that you already hold the key to this place which is none other than the secret Chamber of the Soul, your innermost essence, who has been patiently awaiting you for some time. You become aware of something in your pocket, and delving in, produce a key that fits into the lock.

Thanking Maria, who leaves you now, you walk inside and find yourself into a place like a cave, lit by a single ruby-red lamp. On a throne at one end is seated the figure of a woman who is your *anima,* your soul. Note her appearance and everything about her… You greet each other, and she lets you know how pleased she is that you have come to spend some time with her at last. You ask her what she wants you to do so that your life can become a full expression of your soul, your true self. What is the first, or next, step you must take? Then spend as long as you like in conversation with her – she is very likely to have profound words of wisdom for you...

At this point you have a choice: you can either finish the meditation here or explore the higher chambers, reached by the stone staircase you see spiralling up at the back of this chamber, lit by a dim lantern in the roof.

When it is time to leave, you will find a small door at the back of the cave through which you make your exit. It leads you back into your physical body in this time and place. When you have fully returned, write down the wisdom you learned from your soul.

CHAPTER FIVE

THE ROSE UPON THE CROSS

Who added the roses to the Cross?
The garland of roses swelled, spread on all sides
To surround the hard wood with softness.
Light, silvery clouds soared,
Rose upward with Cross and roses,
And from the centre sprang holy life –
A threefold ray from a single point.
But not a word surrounded the image
To give the mystery sense and clarity.
In the gathering dusk growing grey and greyer,
The pilgrim stood, pondered, and felt himself raised up.
– Goethe, *The Mysteries*[55]

erhaps the greatest, and in many ways, the most mysterious, blooming of the rose took place in the early 17th century with the Rosicrucian Movement, whose symbol is a rose at the centre of a cross. It began in Germany where many Protestants were concerned that the world was in chaos and needed a change of direction. The Reformation had failed to bring about the spiritual renewal that had been hoped for, and Europe was bitterly divided into Catholic and Protestant camps, a stand-off which would eventually lead to the disastrous Thirty Years War. The birth of a new century gave rise to millennial ideals, and the time was ripe for a new age.

THE BROTHERHOOD OF THE ROSY CROSS

In 1610 a clarion call for radical change came in a series of manifestos that were anonymously circulated as pamphlets throughout the town of Kessel. The first of these, *Fama Fraternatis,* (The Proclamation of the Brotherhood) announced the existence of a 'Brotherhood of the Rosy Cross'. It denounced the lack of progress in the 'unthinking world' where scholars were full of pride and ambition, and yet did nothing but squabble over the outdated teachings of philosophers sanctioned by the Church. It condemned religious leaders both East and West – specifying both the Pope and Mahomet – as blasphemers against Jesus Christ. It poured scorn upon alchemists who were only concerned with making gold for material gain rather than seeking 'spiritual' gold. The *Fama* proposed instead a true Reformation, one in which there could be free and open enquiry into the realities of 'God, Man and Nature'. This grand enterprise would draw upon Hermetic, alchemical, Kabbalistic and magical teachings to form the basis for a universal body of spiritual knowledge called *pansophy* (literally, all-wisdom). Science, art, magic, and religion would contribute to a unified cosmology within a harmonious utopian society whose leaders were spiritually illuminated not only through the grace of God but also through the revelations of Nature. The Rosicrucian vision was, in fact, not unlike that of the 'New Age' movement of the West centuries later. Both were seen as imminent due to significant astronomical events around the turn of a century, and both arose from the dismay at the current state of the world and the desire for a new era based on spiritual principles which had their roots in ancient wisdom from a glorious past.

The *Fama* continued to give a fascinating account of the legendary founder of the Brotherhood, Christian Rosencreuz, (Christian Rosy-Cross) who was born in 1378. As a young monk, Brother C.R. travelled to Arabia, Egypt, and Morocco, a journey of initiation on which he learned ancient wisdom from great sages and adepts. On his return he travelled throughout Europe, bursting with enthusiasm to share his new-found knowledge. But instead of the warm reception he expected, he was mocked and reviled by those who feared the new teachings would call their own into doubt and ruin their reputations. Sadly, he returned home to Germany and gathered about him a group who shared his ideals. He began teaching them the wisdom he had learned both from his journey of initiation and also the divinely illuminated insights revealed to him by angels. Thus began the Brotherhood of the Rosy Cross whose base was a building called the 'House of the Holy Spirit'. Their chief work was to travel throughout the land healing the sick free of charge, studying and teaching spiritual knowledge, yet always remaining unobtrusive and anonymous.

According to this legend, Brother C.R. lived to be 106 years old, and was buried in a vault which remained hidden for the next 120 years. Now, however, the vault had been discovered, and within it, the perfectly preserved body of their founder – an event which heralded the dawn of a new age when this hidden wisdom would at last be revealed to a world now ready for a 'general divine and human reformation'.[56]

The *Fama Fraternitatis* included an invitation to interested parties to join the brotherhood. They were to make their intent known either by word of mouth or in writing. Either way, the fraternity would hear of it and make contact with them. Yet although many were inspired to respond, including well-known luminaries such as René Descartes and Elias Ashmole, no-one appears to have received a reply. Nor did the authors ever reveal their identity – anonymity was essential at a time when the Inquisition still held Germany in a grip of terror. Many scholars believe the manifestos to be the work of Johann Valentin Andreae, a young theology student who was part of a group of idealistic philosophers, although it is unlikely that he was the sole author. He is also believed to have been the author of *The Chymical Wedding of Christian Rosenkreutz*, which was published anonymously one year after the manifestos in 1616. In this allegorical fantasy, the narrator, Christian Rosenkreutz, sets forth on a journey of spiritual initiation wearing four red roses in his hat, which he later gives to a beautiful Virgin, a goddess-like figure who acts throughout as his guide and initiator. Andreae's family crest was a St. Andrew's cross with four roses. Later in life Andreae denied the publications were anything more than a playful prank – but by then he had a conservative public position as a Protestant pastor to maintain.

Although the *Fama* and a second pamphlet, *Confessio Fraternitatis*, The Confession of the Brotherhood, published in 1615, professed the continued existence of the original Rosicrucian fraternity, it is very unlikely that they ever existed as a defined group. Nor is there any evidence for the historical existence of their saintly founder. Today it is believed that the 'movement' was a carefully planned piece of allegorical theatre intended as a wake-up call. Its purpose was to inspire people to search for true wisdom that could be found in ancient teachings and the 'Book of Nature', rather than in the ossified dogma of the Church. The pamphlets were meant to act as a catalyst for radical ideological change, preparing Germany for a golden age 'illumined by the hidden light of hermetic wisdom'.[57]

HERMETIC ORIGINS

The Rosicrucian movement was largely fuelled by the esoteric philosophy of Hermeticism, named after the legendary Hermes Trismegistus, 'Thrice-Great Hermes'. This mysterious figure appears to be a fusion of the Greek god, Hermes, and the Egyptian god, Thoth, yet legend also describes him as a great sage from before the time of Moses who brought civilization to Egypt. In fact, the philosophical writings called the *Hermetica* were probably the work of more than one author and date from around the first or second century CE. This was a vibrant period in the history of ideas, when intellectual and religious teachings from many streams, East and West, converged in the great melting-pot

Relief of the Egyptian god Thoth, often depicted as an ibis-headed man, in the temple of Ramses II, Abydos, Egypt

of Alexandria. The texts may have been written as spiritual instructions for students of an initiatic school. They were clearly influenced by the early Gnostics, who believed that a human being is composed of a body, belonging to the material world, and a soul, or divine spark, which is our true spiritual nature. Those seeking enlightenment ever strive to release the spirit from the narrow confines of the body through the path of initiation.

Hundreds of years later, the *Hermetica* were rediscovered and translated by Renaissance scholars in 15th century Italy, who believed the texts hailed from a glorious Golden Age before the Flood. Paradoxically, the discovery of such 'ancient wisdom' proved to be an important key to the future of the modern world. Renaissance thinkers seized upon those ideas which broke the stranglehold of medieval religious beliefs in which man was nothing but a wretched sinner, subservient to God, a powerless pawn in a rigidly ordered universe. In contrast to the Genesis story of the Fall in which Adam and Eve were cast out of Eden for eating from the Tree of Knowledge, the hermetic philosophy taught that the human soul was an immortal spark of the Divine which descended to the physical plane out of love for creation and the desire to use the will and express individual creativity.

Renaissance intellectuals were highly receptive to the concept of the individual as a potent agent of change, one who could learn to unlock the secrets of existence and use that knowledge to serve humanity. Rather than a set of dogmatic religious teachings, Hermeticism offered a method of spiritual evolution, leading to the possibility of attaining gnosis, direct knowledge of the Divine. These exhilarating ideas were supported by the sacred arts of alchemy, astrology, and natural magic, all of which eventually played a major role in shaping modern Western esotericism. However, in the next hundred years, the Catholic Church condemned the Hermetic teachings as heretical, and the new, increasingly dogmatic, Protestant church had no time for them. They were forced underground, until the Rosicrucian Brotherhood revealed them, hence the allegory of the discovery of Christian Rosenkreutz' tomb: his human body was actually a body of teachings, 'perfectly preserved', now brought into the light of day to enlighten a new era.

Although the Rosicrucian vision never materialised in Europe, it sowed seeds which grew into several highly influential movements in the centuries to come, including Freemasonry and the Royal Society in England, which is still one of the most important scientific bodies in the world. More as an inspirational rallying-point than a working order, it caught the imagination of future esotericists, and by the early 20th century, many new Rosicrucian societies

This version of the rose-cross was the emblem of the 19th century
Mystic Order of the Rose + Croix, founded in 1888 in Paris
by Joséphin Péladan and Stanislas de Guaita. It combines the cross,
pentagram, tetragrammaton (four letters of God's name), four
roses, and the Hebrew letter *shin* at the top of the pentagram to
signify the transcendent position of the divine spirit.

and orders, each claiming a connection with the original
founders, sprang up throughout Europe and North
America and are still flourishing today.

As Christopher McIntosh points out:

> *So did the Rosicrucian plan misfire? I think not, because
> this is an interesting example of what happens when you
> plant a mystery in the collective mind of society. It's like
> dropping a stone into a pond: the ripples go on and on.
> And, in this case, the initial impact was so strong that the
> ripples are still going today.*[58]

Ultimately, the essence of the Rose Cross, as envisaged
by its earliest proponents, lies outside of time altogether.

There was no temple, but the 'House of the Holy Spirit', which would remain inaccessible to the godless world,[59] no visible meeting-place, but an 'invisible college' of souls embarked on the spiritual quest – and this is the Rose that will never fade.

THE MEANING OF THE ROSE-CROSS

The rose and the cross are potent, many-layered archetypal symbols, each in their own right. But when the Rosicrucian brotherhood paired the rose with the cross, it was an act of genius that created a third image of unsurpassed beauty and significance. It proved so compelling that many magical orders right down to the present day have taken it as their principal emblem.

The Cross is an ancient symbol that is much older than Christianity. Images of a cross, usually within a circle, have been discovered carved on rocks as early as Paleolithic times in Africa, and on monuments and seals of ancient Sumeria. Circle-crosses on medallions of fine gold leaf have been found on skeletons in megalithic burials in Ireland. Coins and charms from the Bronze Age have been found engraved with the same design. In Vedic India, the sun was represented as a cross and rayed disk.

The circle and the cross are part of the cycle of creation, which proceeds from a point without dimension, the archetypal Sacred Centre. From this centre, the point expands in all directions to become the circle, undifferentiated and whole, the infinite Void or Pleroma, sometimes personified as the womb of the Great Mother. Then unity gives way to polarity as the masculine force arises: the circle is divided by two lines, one of Space and one of Time, resulting in the fourfold pattern that underlies much of the world we live in: the four directions, four tides of the day, four seasons, four elements, four archangels, four worlds in the Kabbalah, and so on. With the advent of the Christian cross, portraying the Roman instrument of torture on which Jesus was crucified, the surrounding circle disappeared, although the early Celtic Christians still used it, and many examples of these beautifully decorated 'High Crosses' can still be found in churchyards throughout Ireland, Scotland, and Wales today.

The loss of the circle in mainstream Christian symbolism paralleled the demotion of the feminine within the Church, but the rose restores the feminine circle to the masculine cross, as it was in ancient times and in the early Celtic church. In Chapter Two, we saw how the Feminine entered into sacred Christian art and poetry in the Middle Ages with the Virgin Mary in her rose garden. In the 17th century the Rosicrucians restored the rose to its full glory in the centre of human life by pairing it with the cross.

In the Christian context of the original founders of the Rosicrucian movement, the rose is viewed as the Christ-Spirit dwelling in the soul. They emphasised the risen Christ, rather than the crucifixion, as evidenced by the central Rosicrucian dictum:

Ex deo nascimur,
in Jesu morimur,
per Spiritum Sanctum reviviscimus

From God we are born,
in Jesus we die,
through the Holy Spirit we live again.

Influenced by Renaissance humanism, the symbol points the way to the spiritual rebirth of the individual – the soul emerging from the human personality to experience spiritual illumination; higher consciousness unfolding its petals within the human heart. This shows a significant development in meaning from the medieval Marian cult, in which the rose is associated with a semi-divine figure *outside* of ourselves.

'Harmonious Conception of the Light of Nature' from *Secret Symbols of the Rosicrucians* by unknown 18th century German compiler.

Esoteric scholar A.E. Waite comments: 'The Solar Rose is centred in the glory of the Sun and the Christ of Nazareth is centred in the celestial flower. . . In the deep understanding of Rosicrucian doctrine, the Rose is also the Soul and Christ is the Indwelling Spirit.'

Symbolic of the spiritual quest of the individual, the cross represents human existence in the world of space-time, the 'cross of initiation' on which we are bound for a multitude of lifetimes. It also speaks of the sacrifice (crucifixion) of the conditioned self that must be made so that the rose of the soul can blossom within the heart. As alchemist and physician, Michael Maier, wrote: 'To live amidst Roses and under a Cross are contrary things – joy and sorrow'.[60]

The rose and the cross together harmonise and unify the opposites, reconciling heaven with earth, above with below. The Rose of Spirit blooming on the fourfold elemental cross becomes the *quintessence* or fifth element in the centre of the cross, signifying Spirit. If the cross is laid flat, and the Rose elevated above it, the flower forms the tip of the pyramid. Its fourfold pattern is a reminder of the harmony and balance of all things: four dancing gods and goddesses that weave their steps into the spiral patterning of time and space, returning time and time again into the heart of the Rose to be renewed, then bursting forth to tread their merry measures once again, while the Rose blossoms eternally on the Tree of Life.

H. Spencer Lewis, founder of the 20th century Rosicrucian order, AMORC (Ancient and Mystical Order Rosae Crucis) wrote:

The rose as a flower was considered in many oriental lands as a sacred and divine manifestation through nature and the process of its unfolding and development seem to symbolise the unfolding and development of the soul. Its beauty, rare fragrance, tenderness, sweetness, magnificence of colour,

rarity, and other qualities, helped to make it symbolical of
the soul of man. The joining of these two then, the rose
and the cross, is the logical unity of two outstanding sacred
principles – the physical body of man and the delicate
unfolding soul nature within.[61]

The petals of the rose unfold within the human heart to reveal the divine spark – the glowing centre which opens to receive the rays of the great spiritual Sun. This innermost heart of the rose is the divine centre of all being, which lies beyond space and time. It celebrates the awakened soul that has evolved beyond identification with the world of duality and knows itself to be one with Spirit. Yet it manifests within the body in order to share the exquisite fragrance and beauty of the rose with the world. For the rose-cross symbolises both the journey to heaven that takes the seeker from the cross to the rose, then returns to Earth to bring the wisdom of higher consciousness to all of humanity.

In 1629, a unique version of the Rose Cross appeared on the cover of a book, Summum Bonum, a defence of the Rosicrucians by Robert Fludd, a 17th century English physician, philosopher and alchemist.[62] The stylised rose blossom is composed of seven circles of seven petals, above which are the words, Dat Rosa Mel Apibus – the rose gives honey to the bees. The blossom is oversized, while the stem is formed in the shape of a cross, symbolising the supremacy of the circle of spirit over the cross of matter. Together blossom and stem form the astrological sign of the planet Venus, whose magic number is seven. In early Hermetic teachings seven is associated with the number of planets and the stages of the soul's ascent on its return to God.

*To the right is a hive of bees, two of whom have reached
the rose. In the background on the left is a four-square
grape arbour fence, on which a spider has spun a web, also
in seven circuits. The number four signifies the physical
plane, whilst the grapevine has been a symbol of abundance
and life from ancient times through the time of Christ.
Transcending the thorny challenges of life, the bees approach
the nectar within the Rose of Spirit. Yet their job does not
end in mystical communion with the rose, but rather with
the return to the hive to transform the pollen into honey
for the good of the whole, just as, in the Western esoteric
tradition, the goal of the Work is service to all.*

MEDITATION V –
EMBODYING THE ROSE
ON THE CROSS

You can keep your eyes open or closed during this meditation. It can be done standing or sitting.

Relax and take a few deep breaths. With each exhalation, visualise your feet extending deep down into the Earth. As they make contact with the centre of the planet, feel a strong wave of Earth energy coursing up from below into your feet, then streaming up your spine all the way to the top of your head where it shoots out into the vastness of the cosmos. And from the highest point of the heavens, the supernal energy of Light and Love pours down through your spine. This flowing current that connects Earth with Sky in Space continues effortlessly, cleansing, purifying, and connecting you with the radiant power of the Above and Below...

Now focus on your heart centre and become aware of a horizontal line of energy bisecting the vertical current and streaming out in both directions to infinity. This is the current of Time which forms the boundary of the temporal dimension in which we live, flowing constantly and inexorably from past to present to future...

Space and Time converge at your heart centre where your human self lives, moves, and has its being in the present moment. Feel this stillpoint that is the eternal Now...

Now breathe gently into your heart centre and allow an image of a rosebud to emerge. The rosebud is closed, tightly encased within its protective green sepals. But as it is warmed by the spiritual Sun above and energised by the green fire of the Earth from below, the sepals slowly begin to unfurl, revealing the delicate petals within...

As they do so, you become aware of a blossoming also occurring in the depths of your being. You feel that something in you is opening and coming to light...

As you continue to take deep breaths, the petals unfurl one by one as they drink in the life-giving Light from Above and Below. With each inhalation, you absorb its fragrance into your being...

Gaze into the glowing, golden heart of the Rose and let its beauty and perfume fill your mind with a sense of peace and bliss. Rest in this space as long as you can, continuing with the gentle breath...

It's also possible that an image begins to emerge. This image represents whatever is most beautiful, most meaningful and most creative that wants to come to light in your life right now. Stay with this image for some time and absorb its quality. Sense what it means for you and open to receive the gift...

When you are ready, allow your breathing to return to normal, and let all images slowly fade away...

Open your eyes and write down your thoughts and feelings.

CHAPTER SIX

ROSES OF A GOLDEN DAWN

he symbol of the rose and cross continued to be a source of inspiration long after the original Rosicrucian manifestos appeared. Although there may never have been a real-life 'Rosicrucian brotherhood', the 18th and 19th centuries saw the proliferation of several groups using the name. Many of them were part of the burgeoning speculative Freemasonry movement, which had its own 'Rose-Croix of Heredom' initiation rite. One of these groups, the Rosicrucian Society in England, (*Societas Rosicruciana in Anglia,* or SRIA) was to have a profound influence on the 19th century occult revival. In 1887, three of its members founded a magical society called the Hermetic Order of the Golden Dawn, which became the foremost esoteric society of the 20th century, whose offshoots are still active today. Membership, which included women as well as men, was drawn closely from the English middle classes, particularly intellectuals and artists. As with the original Rosicrucian impulse, the beginning of a new century inspired many to join a movement which promised a new, spiritually enlightened age. Indeed, although it had a relatively short life, the Golden Dawn has done more than any other order to ensure the continuation of a vital current of Western esotericism in the modern world.

CEREMONIES AND INITIATIONS

The Golden Dawn provided teachings in the theory and practice of the classic Rosicrucian subjects, including Qabalah, alchemy, tarot, and astrology. Yet its far-ranging syncretism also included material from Egyptian, Hindu, Buddhist, and Greek sources. For example, the rose-cross was seen both as a Christian symbol and as the *crux ansata,* or *ankh,* the Egyptian symbol of life. The aim of the order was to help individuals evolve spiritually and awaken to a higher state of consciousness through making contact with their Higher Self, or Holy Guardian Angel, for their personal evolution and in service to the world. Each member advanced by proceeding through a series of grades based upon an ascent through the *sephiroth,* or stations on the Qabalistic Tree of Life, their progress marked by dramatic ceremonies of initiation. The Rose was an important symbol throughout all these rituals. A red rose was placed on the altar for the Neophyte Ceremony, while in the later Portal Ceremony, the altar was adorned with rose leaves.

After mastering the first four grades, in which they studied the theory of magic, they could apply for admission to the inner order called the *Ordo Rosae Rubeae et Aureae Crucis*, the Order of the Ruby Rose and the Gold Cross, (R. R. et A. C.). This would mark their graduation to the rank of Adeptus Minor where they learned meditations, rituals,

Ceiling and floor designs of the Vault of the Adepts. On the floor below, the same heptagonal figure was interwoven with a seven-headed dragon which represented the unregenerate lower forces within the psyche of the candidate, now conquered and trodden underfoot. In the centre, within a downward-pointing triangle, was the 'Rescuing Symbol of the Golden Cross united to the Red Rose of Seven times Seven Petals'.

exercises, and other magical practices. Candidates had to take part in a spectacularly dramatic initiation ceremony created by one of the founders, Samuel MacGregor Mathers, a charismatic writer and ceremonialist, and his brilliant artist wife and priestess, Moina. A special seven-sided room was constructed within the temple to represent the tomb of Christian Rosenkreuz, the mythical founder of the order. It was also called the Vault of the Adepts and the Tomb of Osiris and was to be imagined as lying within a secret chamber at the centre of the Rosicrucian Mount of Initiation. Each of the inner walls was decorated with qabalistic, alchemical, and astrological symbols in colours designed to have a consciousness-altering effect.

In the centre of the ceiling, set within an upward-pointing triangle, was painted a white rose with twenty-two petals: the number of letters in the Hebrew alphabet, paths in the Tree of Life and tarot trumps. This was surrounded by a seven-sided figure and symbolised the supernal Light.

During the initiation ceremony, the candidate was put through a series of ritual trials, including being bound to a cross, to learn the values of humility, self-sacrifice and service. The Chief Adept, or acting priest, lay in a *pastos,* or coffin beneath the altar, as Christian Rosenkreuz, to represent the aspirant's higher self, hidden and confined within the personality. At the climax of the ceremony the priest arose from the coffin as the candidate's newly awakened spiritual self. Israel Regardie, a member of the Golden Dawn who published their ceremonies, wrote of this ritual:

> *The whole concatenation of symbols is an elaborate and dramatic portrayal of the central theme of the Great Work. In a word, it depicts the spiritual rebirth or redemption of the candidate, his resurrection from the dark tomb of mortality through the power of the holy Spirit.*[63]

The Rose Cross Lamen

The newly initiated Adeptus Minor had to make and consecrate a series of symbolic magical tools. The most important of these was a personal lamen, or pendant, to be worn over the heart, depicting the 'complete symbol' of the order. [64]

The Rose Cross Lamen

In the centre is the five petalled red rose with a luminous white central point which represents the highest sephirah of Kether, the Crown on the Qabalistic Tree of Life that emanates supernal Light. It is set on a gold Calvary cross, a figure which can be folded up to make a cube, the sign of Earth. The centre of the rose is surrounded by three concentric circles, also seen as petals. The first circle contains the three Mother Letters of the Hebrew alphabet, followed by the seven double and twelve simple letters, totalling twenty-two, for the twenty-two paths on the Tree of Life.

The arms of the outer Calvary cross are in the traditional colours of the four elements: Air – yellow, Fire – red, Water – blue, Earth, which in Western magic became citrine, olive, russet and black. Each one contains a pentagram and the alchemical symbols for mercury, sulphur, and salt, representing spirit, soul and body. The pentagram is a sacred symbol used extensively in Golden Dawn rituals. It represents the four elements topped by the fifth one, the quintessence: Spirit. On the lower arm is a hexagram surrounded by glyphs of the seven planets, with the sun in the middle. The hexagram is also a highly important symbol: it is composed of the two interlocking triangles of Fire and Water and represents the marriage of the Above with the Below. It is also associated with the sixth sephirah of Tiphareth on the Tree of Life, the central sphere between Heaven and Earth, where the Higher Self resides. The white rays at the angles of the cross are seen as rays of divine light streaming from the centre of the rose, as the reflected heavenly light of Kether. The largest four spell the letters of the acronym, I.N.R.I., which has many layers of meaning from Christian, alchemical and Egyptian sources, and is used in rituals of transformation.
Of this figure, Israel Regardie says:

The Rose-Cross is a Lamen or badge synthesizing a vast concourse of ideas, representing in a single emblem the Great Work itself—the harmonious reconciliation in one symbol of diverse and apparently contradictory concepts, the reconciliation of divinity and manhood. It is a highly important symbol to be worn over the heart during every important operation. It is a glyph, in one sense, of the higher Genius to whose knowledge and conversation the student is eternally aspiring. In the Rituals it is described as the Key of Sigils and Rituals.[65]

115

One of the most prominent members of the Golden Dawn was poet and mystic, Arthur Edward Waite. The Rose was central to the symbolism he used in all aspects of his work. A self-taught scholar of Christianity and medieval Kabbalism, Waite viewed the Rose as both Mary and the Shekinah:

> *Thus the Rose is a symbol of Mary because of her motherhood, but in relation to her it belongs to divine things, even as she herself stands on the threshold of Deity, being Spouse of the Divine Spirit and bearer of the Divine word made flesh. So also is the Rose of Shekinah, a Divine Rose, as she whom it typifies is Divine Mother of souls.* [66]

Waite was more drawn to mystical Christianity than magic, and eventually left the Golden Dawn to found his own sacramental Christian order, which he called the Fellowship of the Rosy Cross. The initiation rituals he wrote for the Fellowship combine elements from masonic, Qabalistic, and alchemical teachings, and his use of the Rose stands as a beautiful example of the way a numinous symbol of the highest potency can be used to transmit its spiritual force through the medium of ritual.

In a first-grade ritual of his order a 'Sacramental Rose' is placed upon the altar which is held up to the words: 'The mind which looks to Thee is a Rose that unfolds in Thy Light.' The 'Guide of the Paths' says:

> *This Rose also shall pass through to you, and you shall receive it from my hands, a sign of the bond of union between the worlds above and below.*

The Sacramental Rose was then passed around to each member, along with a lamp signifying the Divine Light. Waite brought red and white roses into the temple to symbolise the pair of higher sephiroth on the Qabalistic Tree of Life known as Justice and Mercy. In another ritual, red, white, and blush roses were laid on the altar to signify the alchemical marriage of the opposites and the birth of a new divine 'child'. A prayer from one of his ceremonies was uttered:

In the Name of Thy Holy Shekinah and by the union of red and white in the Mystical Rose of benignity, awaken us to the life that is eternal.[67]

The following excerpt is taken from the Fellowship's 'Ceremony of Consecration on the Threshold of Sacred Mystery for the Watchers of the Holy House'. The temple is dark except for a large Rose Cross which appears in mid-air as if suspended in the darkness. The fragrance of incense rises from thuribles, while music plays in the background.

The High Priest: *The Tree of the Rosy Cross is Christ; the Tree is Life; the Tree is the Word made flesh; Immanuel, God is with us. It is also the manifested state of our humanity; and then the Rose signifies the Immanent Divinity, Which dwells within us, at once hidden and revealed. I bear my witness further that the Rose is the soul in man; and then the glittering point of dew, as the jewel within the centre, is the inward and hidden Christhood…*

A voice of song tells of the Mystic Rose.

The Priestess of the Rite: *Rosa Aurea, Rosa Sancta, Rosa Victoriae, Rosa Mystica, Rosa Immortalis, Rosa Coeli, Rosa Foederis, Rosa Sanctissima, Rosa Deitatis, Rosa Salutaris Nostrae, Rosa Unitatis, O Purissima, O Sanctissima, Dulcis Rosa Christi… The Rose art Thou, and we are the Rose in Thee: we are also a chaplet of roses about Thy morning Star. The flower of the field is mine and this is the Holy Rose: I have bound Thy lilies on my heart. My Rose expands in Thy light. The dew of Thy Presence formed therein, and it breathes forth fragrance of the Spirit. O Rosa Florescens.*[68]

The founders of the original Rosicrucian Brotherhood would surely have approved of Waite's beautiful ceremonies which bring together the archetypal meanings of the Rose and the Cross – even though they would not have dared perform such rites openly three hundred years ago.

Tarot cards played an important part in the initiatory work of the Golden Dawn. The tarot first appeared in the 14th century as a card game in France and Italy. It was not considered to have any esoteric significance until four hundred years later, when Swiss pastor and freemason, Antoine Court de Gébelin, claimed that the images encoded the lost wisdom of ancient Egypt, as taught by the god, Thoth, another name for Hermes. These ideas were developed by the highly influential French magician, Eliphas Lévi, in the 19th century, who linked the cards with the Qabala, alchemy and ceremonial magic. His system was taken up by the Golden Dawn, and in 1909, Waite created the deck which sparked the 20th century renaissance of the tarot and is still accepted as the standard today.

The images on the Rider-Waite-Smith deck, as it is now known, are richly symbolic. Roses appear in several cards, especially the trumps, which came to be known as the Major Arcana. This is not surprising, since Waite, as we have seen, came to identify himself as a Christian Rosicrucian.

The Fool

This is the first card in the deck, numbered zero. In the accompanying booklet, 'A Pictorial Key to the Tarot', Waite described this figure as 'spirit in search of experience'. He calls him

THE FOOL.

The Fool

> . . . *a prince of the other world on his travels through this one – all amidst the morning glory, in the keen air. The sun, which shines behind him, knows whence he came, whither he is going, and how he will return by another path after many days.*[69]

The Fool, then, is the human soul, preparing for a cycle of experience on Earth. He has descended from the heavenly heights of the mountains behind him and is about to step off into the 'fallen' world below. His purity and innocence is expressed by his light and graceful posture, and his face upturned in confident anticipation, while the little white dog, the instinctual self, bounds eagerly by his side. In his right hand, the side of practical action, he holds the staff of the personal will, topped by a bag of provisions – his resources for the journey. In his left hand, the inward intuitive side, he holds aloft a white rose, which signifies the guiding wisdom of the spirit world, which will support him on his journey through life.

The Magician

In the next card in the series, I, The Magician, the figure is well and truly centred in the physical world. Like the Fool, he bears a masculine object, a wand, in his right hand, but in contrast, his left hand is pointing down towards Earth, as he mediates the Above to the Below, bringing Spirit into Form. The wand and the other three implements on the table are symbols of the four elements of which the physical world is composed. The Magician

The Magician

works beneath an arbour of red roses, while more spring up at his feet. Red is the colour of the physical world, of fire and of blood. Here they contrast with the white lilies, a flower associated with the purity of the heaven world. The alchemical symbolism is very clear in this card: the Magician is a skilled alchemist, actively balancing the opposites and integrating Heaven and Earth.

The Empress

The Empress

A stately woman dressed in a flowing white gown covered with large red roses provides the image The Empress, numbered III. The heart-shaped shield on her right side shows us that we are once more in the presence of Venus/Aphrodite. She wears a crown of twelve stars and bears a sceptre topped with a globe to show her rulership of the Earth. Before her is a field of ripening grain, while behind are verdant woods and a waterfall. The red roses speak of her beauty, love, and fruitful creativity in the earthly plane.

Strength

In card VIII, Strength, a serenely beautiful woman is closing the mouth of a lion in a firm yet gentle gesture. She wears a garland of roses around her waist, and although it is not visible in the picture, Waite writes that she is leading the subdued lion by a chain of flowers. The woman demonstrates how one who is spiritually evolved can gain mastery of their lower instincts. She is clothed in white, while the roses are red, for she has integrated spiritual wisdom into her earthly life.

Strength

Death

Perhaps the most dramatic rose is found on card XIII, Death. A skeleton in black armour bears a banner with a large five-petalled white rose on a black background. He is Death, one of the four riders of the Apocalypse, and as he rides his white horse through the landscape, young and old, rich and poor alike, fall dead before him. The dead and dying wear the red roses of the earthly plane which drop to the ground. They contrast with the white rose, which Waite describes as 'the Mystic Rose, which signifies life'. The imagery recalls the Vault of the Adepti ceremony, with its white rose on the ceiling, and red rose on the floor. In the background, a golden sun rises between the two pillars of the opposites, to emphasize that Death is not the end of life, but 'rebirth, creation, destination, renewal'.[70]

Death

In these classic cards that served as the template for many modern decks to come, the parallel with the alchemical emblems of the Rose is hard to ignore: Throughout the centuries the collective Western psyche continually struggles for a way to balance and unite the opposites in its search for harmony and peace and ultimately, the unity which transcends them.

MEDITATION VI –
THE MOUNT OF INITIATION

One of the Golden Dawn's most famous members was the poet, W. B. Yeats. According to his biographer, Richard Ellman, Yeats 'was particularly moved by the central myth of the Golden Dawn which was the mystical death and resurrection of the adept'.[71] In 1909 he wrote a meditation centred around Mount of Abniegus, the Rosicrucian Mount of Initiation, based on the Golden Dawn's ritual of the Adeptus Minor. The following is a slightly adapted version of the original script.

Close your eyes and take some long, slow, deep breaths, letting go of all outer concerns. See yourself walking on a path through a deep, silent forest at nightfall. The only guiding light you have comes from Venus, the evening star: the heavenly lamp that lights the path ahead for the initiate...

The path begins to slope uphill, the trees thin out, and you find yourself walking up a mountainside. This is the central mountain of the world; its top is flat and encircled by a walled garden. This is the Garden of Eden. The birds of the night cry one by one. You can go no further but are lost among confused cries of birds in the gathering darkness.

You pray for more light and suddenly a cave appears before you, its mouth shining with light. You walk into the cave. It has seven sides and the walls are carved with Egyptian or earlier figures. In the middle of the cave is a sarcophagus. You spread your arms out to the sides in the shape of a cross, then lie down in it. . As you do so, three figures draw near, one of whom places a rose on your breast. The second one places a wand in your right hand and a lotus in your left. You gaze upward at the Rose and say, 'O Rose of Rubies grant to me the knowledge of seven earth keys and the power over these. Let me know what I have been – what I am and what I shall become!' Then think of yourself as passing into deep sleep, and as you start to lose consciousness, cry out, 'O Rose take me up into thy joy.' Envisage your soul ascending into a world of light and knowledge where the meaning of your life will become clear. Rise up the mountain and enter the Garden of Eden ...

Spend as much time here as you choose. When you wish to return to ordinary consciousness, allow all images to fade, take some deep breaths and return. Take some moments to write down your experiences.

CHAPTER SEVEN

THE SECRET ROSE OF
W.B. YEATS

Surely thine hour has come, thy great wind blows,
Far off, most secret, and inviolate Rose?
– W.B.Yeats, To the Secret Rose

he magical Rose of the Golden Dawn was taken to Ireland by one of its most illustrious members. In 1890 William Butler Yeats met MacGregor Mathers in the reading room of the British Museum and, impressed by his magical powers, joined the order. In 1893 he was initiated into the inner order, where he would have learned the full significance of the Rose Cross symbol. He played an active part in running the organisation, including helping Mathers write rituals and initiation ceremonies. In 1900 he became the Imperator of the Isis-Urania Temple in London. When, after a series of scandals, the order changed its name to Stella Matutina in 1901, he acted as Imperator of the Amoun Temple from 1914 to 1922, when he withdrew from the order altogether.

Yeats' dedication to occult studies and magical practice informed his life and work on all levels. He wrote: … If I had not made magic my constant study I could not have written a single word …The mystical life is the centre of all that I do and all that I think and all that I write. . . I have all ways considered myself a voice of what I believe to be a greater renaissance – the revolt of the soul against the intellect – now beginning in the world.[72]

Yeats considered himself part of the Symbolist Movement of avant-garde artists, writers, and musicians in the late 19th century. Rebelling against the rationalism and materialism of the age, they believed that true art was based on spiritual experience, imagination, and dreams. A leading light of the movement was the colourful French novelist and art critic, Joséphin Péladan, founder of the Rosicrucian secret society, The Mystic Order of the Rose + Croix. Yeats believed that art was a vehicle for the expression of spiritual ideas, which he thought of as 'the world of essences', in which the artist was priest. He wrote:

The arts are, I believe, about to take upon their shoulders the burdens that had fallen from the shoulders of priests, and to lead us back upon our journey by filling our thoughts with the essences of things, and not with things.[73]

ETERNAL ROSE OF BEAUTY

The image he used most in his early work to symbolise 'the essence of things' was the Rose, which rambles through his poetry and prose as an emblem of eternal beauty and transcendental love.[74] In a note to a group of shorter poems, called simply *The Rose*, he declared that in them the writer had found, 'the only pathway whereon he can hope to see with his own eyes the "Eternal Rose of Beauty and of Peace."' [75] The rose-cross was particularly important to him as it symbolises the tension between time and eternity, mortal and immortal, a consistent theme throughout his poetry. The opening poem bears the title, *To the Rose upon the Rood of Time*. Yeats prays to the Rose to draw near so that he may discover the unchanging spiritual world of 'eternal beauty' that lies beneath the mortal world of desire:

> *Red Rose, proud Rose, sad Rose of all my days!*
> *Come near me, while I sing the ancient ways:*
> *. . . Come near, that no more blinded by man's fate,*
> *I find under the boughs of love and hate,*
> *In all poor foolish things that live a day,*
> *Eternal beauty wandering on her way.*[76]

True to the Rosicrucian spirit, Yeats does not seek the divine only in the non-physical realm but asks that his eyes may be opened to see the infinite as it is expressed in the temporal world. Although he had experimented with Theosophy for a while, Yeats rejected the Eastern path of transcendence, and found his true path in Western esoteric tradition, with its emphasis on the individual as a mediator between Heaven and Earth. Florence Farr, his friend and colleague in the Golden Dawn, defined this as the adept's decision 'to choose a life that shall bring him in touch with the sorrows of his race rather than accept the Nirvana open to him; and like other Saviours of the world, to remain manifested as a living link between the supernal and terrestrial natures.'[77] In the second stanza of this poem, he makes it clear he does not seek an absolute union with the eternal, but asks the Rose to help him find poetic inspiration in everyday life:

> *Come near, come near, come near—Ah, leave me still*
> *A little space for the Rose-breath to fill!*
> *Lest I no more hear common things that crave;*
> *The weak worm hiding down in its small cave,*
> *...The field-mouse running by me in the grass,*
> *And heavy mortal hopes that toil and pass;* [78]

Yeats saw the tension between the opposites as providing the friction that sparked life into art. In a later essay on poetry and tradition, he was to write:

> *...the nobleness of the arts is in the mingling of the contraries, the extremity of sorrow, the extremity of joy, perfection of personality, the perfection of its surrender, overflowing turbulent energy, and marmorean stillness; and its red rose opens at the meeting of the two beams of the cross, and at the trysting-place of mortal and immortal, time and eternity.*[79]

THE ROSE UPON THE TREE

In a note to some of his early poems, Yeats described the Rose as the 'principal symbol of the divine nature' in the West, which replaced the Lotus of the East:

> *Because the Rose, the flower sacred to the Virgin Mary and the flower that Apuleius' adventurer ate, when he*

was changed out of the ass's shape and received into the Fellowship of Isis, is the western Flower of Life, I have imagined it growing upon the Tree of Life.

I once stood beside a man in Ireland when he saw it growing there in a vision, that seemed to have rapt him out of his body. He saw the garden of Eden walled about, and in the top of a high mountain, as in certain mediaeval diagrams, and after passing the Tree of Knowledge, on which grew fruit full of troubled faces, and through those branches flowed, he was told, sap that was human souls, he came to a tall dark tree, with little bitter fruits, and was shown a kind of stair or ladder going up through the tree, and told to go up; and near the top of the tree, a beautiful woman, like the Goddess of Life associated with the tree in Assyria, gave him a rose that seemed to have been growing upon the tree.[80]

For Yeats, as for Waite, the Rose expressed the eternal beauty of the spirit world: a gift from the Divine Feminine bestowed upon those willing to endure the 'bitter fruits' of self-abnegation, and gain knowledge of higher realities by ascending the Qabalistic Tree of Life.[81]

In one of these poems, *The Poet Pleads with the Elemental Powers,* Yeats laments that the Rose has been torn from the Tree. The poem begins:

The Powers whose name and shape no living creature knows
Have pulled the Immortal Rose;
And though the Seven Lights bowed in their dance and wept,
The Polar Dragon slept,
His heavy rings uncoiled from glimmering deep to deep:
When will he wake from sleep? [82]

Of this poem, Yeats says:

> *I have made the Seven Lights, the Constellation of the Bear, lament for the theft of the Rose, and I have made the Dragon, the constellation Draco, the guardian of the Rose, because these constellations move about the pole of the heavens, the ancient Tree of Life in many countries, and are often associated with the Tree of Life in mythology.* [83]

The striking imagery recalls the early Gnostic account of the Fall and is clearly influenced from Yeats' esoteric training. It also has echoes of William Blake's cosmological poems, in which the 'lapsèd soul' is seen as having its origins in 'the starry pole'.[84]

THE ROSE OF IRELAND

Yeats was not content to be writing about an Assyrian goddess on the Tree of Life, but searched for the Rose in Irish mythology, revealing his other great theme of this time which was to 'Sing of old Eire and the ancient ways.' He made connections between the rose of antiquity and pre-Christian Celtic religion:

> *I have read somewhere that a stone engraved with a Celtic god, who holds what looks like a rose in one hand, has been found somewhere in England; ... If the Rose was really a symbol of Ireland among the Gaelic poets ... one may feel pretty certain that the ancient Celts associated the Rose with Eire, or Fotla, or Banba—goddesses who gave their names to Ireland—or with some principal god or goddess, for such symbols are not suddenly adopted or invented but come out of mythology.* [85]

Yeats' great dream was to develop an artistic and spiritual revival that would parallel Ireland's independence from British oppression, which was seen as a real possibility as the century drew to a close. Many of his early poems, stories, and plays are drawn from Celtic mythology, folk and fairy tales, which he saw as arising out of the very soul of Ireland. From his time spent among the peasantry in the West of Ireland, he saw that the ancient Celtic myths were still alive in the hearts and minds of the people, like a smouldering flame that his words could stir into life. By reviving and reworking the archetypal themes of his native land, he envisaged a cultural renaissance in which 'the Saxon empire of realism and materialism might be encircled and destroyed'.

CASTLE OF HEROES

Combining his twin passions for magic and the liberation of Ireland, Yeats was inspired to create a secret society based on the Irish Mysteries. He hoped that while his literary work would transform mainstream culture, behind it would lie a hidden, magical 'inner order' whose adepts would work on spiritually strengthening the movement for the Irish cause. For Yeats, this became an obsession stronger than anything else in his life, and in 1895 he found the perfect base for the order – an abandoned castle on a small island in the middle of Lough Key, County Roscommon. He called it the 'Castle of Heroes' and his plan was to turn it into the headquarters of what would be called the Celtic Mystical Order.

He enlisted the support of many of the luminaries of the Celtic Revival including visionary poet George Russell, known as A.E., and Scottish author, William Sharp, who both contributed material for rites and ceremonies. Their

Castle Island in Lough Key, County Roscommon, Ireland:
the setting for Yeats' Castle of Heroes

aim was to call up the ancient, archetypal forces of the land, to rouse its gods, goddesses and heroes for Ireland's renewal at the deepest level. In this he was encouraged by the visions of A.E. who announced in a letter to Yeats, 1896, that 'the gods have returned to Erin and have centred themselves in the sacred mountains and blow the fires through the country. They have been seen by several in vision. They will awaken the magical instinct everywhere, and the universal heart of the people will turn to the old Druidic beliefs . . . Out of Ireland will arrive a light to transform many ages and peoples.'[86]

Yeats also believed that a new global era was about to begin, in which not only Ireland, but the whole world would experience transformation on all levels. He wrote:

> *I cannot get it out of my head that this age of criticism is about to pass, and an age of imagination, of emotion, of revelation, about to come in its place; for certainly a belief in a supersensual world is at hand again. . .*[87]

Like the original Rosicrucians, Yeats used the Rose as a symbol of hope for a coming 'Golden Dawn' in a new century. Like them, he was influenced by the prophesies of 12th century theologian, Joachim de Fiore, foretelling the coming of an 'Age of the Holy Spirit'[88] which would bring about a universal dispensation of love and peace. He hoped that the Celtic Mystical Order would play a leading role in the coming changes, and 'would unite the radical truth of Christianity to those of a more ancient world.'[89] A.E. believed this would be the inevitable result of the Piscean Age giving way to the Age of Aquarius, an oft-quoted maxim of the current New Age movement. In the poem, *The Secret Rose*, Yeats expresses this hope to the Rose, here seen as a force that will bring about sweeping changes in the world:

> *Surely thine hour has come, thy great wind blows,*
> *Far-off, most secret, and inviolate Rose?*[90]

Yeats also had another motive for creating his magical order. At the time, he was deeply in love with actress and revolutionary, Maud Gonne, who was fervently committed to the nationalist cause. Although she never returned his devotion, they were to come together in a spiritual partnership that dominated the rest of the poet's life. In several of his early poems, the Rose refers to his love for Maud, as for instance in *The Lover Tells of the Rose in his Heart*, in which he describes how her image 'blossoms a rose in the deeps of my heart'. Maud's presence can also be felt in a sequence of poems from *The Rose*, including, *The Rose of Battle, The Rose of Peace*, and *The Rose of the World*.

William Yeats and Maud Gonne

As they worked side by side on the Castle of Heroes project, Yeats hoped he would finally win Maud's love, and that they would act together as priest and priestess to 'establish mysteries like those of Eleusis or Samothrace'. Maud used her not inconsiderable visionary skills to make contact with the Irish gods and goddesses known as the Tuatha Dé Danann for spiritual guidance. But she was unable to accept Yeats' lack of political engagement, which he defended in a poem, *To Ireland in the Coming Times*. Yeats argued that, just because he focused on mythological and spiritual realities, he was no less patriotic than those poets whose theme was the struggle for Irish independence:

Know, that I would accounted be
True brother of a company
That sang, to sweeten Ireland's wrong,
Ballad and story, rann and song; [91]

However, Maud was not convinced of the value of poetry over praxis, and the Castle of Heroes project never came to fruition. This was at least partly due to her marriage in 1903 to Irish Nationalist, Sean McBride, which threw Yeats into a profound depression. Bitterly disappointed, he turned his attention and energy to founding the Abbey Theatre in Dublin, hoping his plays would help bring about the Irish literary renaissance he dreamed of. Indeed much of the material that came out of the magical order provided the basis for his plays, so it has been truly said that Irish drama was born out of the ashes of the Celtic Mysteries. Although as Maud said, the Castle of Heroes was to remain a castle in the air, Yeats would remark on the occasion of their last meeting before his death, 'Maud, we should have gone on with our Castle of the Heroes, we might still do it!'

ROSA ALCHEMICA

Yeats even created a fictional magical society called 'The Order of the Alchemical Rose' in a book of symbolist short stories published in 1897. This collection was titled, *The Secret Rose,* and the poem of that name was used at the opening of the book, like a powerful invocation before a magical working. This was no mere literary device: Steven Putzel explains:

> *Rather than being purely a work of literature, he looked upon this book as 'an arcane text and an outline of a symbolic mytho-historic system, designed to prepare new members of the Hermetic Order of the Golden Dawn for magical work.'*[92]

In the story, *Rosa Alchemica,* the narrator is an aesthetic young man, Owen Aherne, who lives a closeted life surrounded by his collection of beautiful art and artefacts. They give him little pleasure because he is afraid to engage fully in the passions they portray, although he longs for 'a world made wholly of essences'. He has even added a set of alchemical apparatus to his collection, inspired by 'the supreme dream of the alchemist, the transmutation of the weary heart into a weariless spirit', yet he is unable to commit himself to the alchemist's path wherein 'all must be dissolved before the divine substance, material gold or immaterial ecstasy, awake.'[93]

He is rescued from this life of emotional and spiritual paralysis by Michael Robartes, a magician whose fiery magnetic personality was based on MacGregor Mathers. Robartes invites him to become initiated in the Order of the Alchemical Rose and takes him to its temple on the edge of the wild and windswept western sea. He is prepared for his initiation by being robed in crimson (for 'passion') and given 'a little chainless censer of bronze, wrought into the likeness of a rose'.[94] He is then led into a great circular room decorated lavishly with images of divine figures. A mosaic of an immense rose adorns the ceiling.

Men and women, dressed in crimson robes, are moving to the sound of hidden instruments in a slow dance, which Aherne is encouraged to join. He soon realises that the steps of the dancers are tracing the shapes of the rose petals above. On the floor of the chamber Aherne sees that 'a pale Christ on a pale cross was wrought in the midst'. When he asks Robartes the meaning of this, he is told 'that they desired "To trouble His unity with their multitudinous feet."' In other words, the bloodless monotheism of Christianity must be transformed by the rose whose petals are the living forces of the Immortals, come down to Earth to revitalize human life.

The music begins to speed up and as the dancers whirl around, Aherne sinks into a trance-like dream in which he sees an extraordinary sight:

> *I was awakened by seeing the petals of the great rose, which had no longer the look of mosaic, falling slowly through the incense-heavy air, and, as they fell, shaping into the likeness of living beings of an extraordinary beauty. Still faint and cloud-like, they began to dance, and as they danced took a more and more definite shape, so that I was able to distinguish beautiful Grecian faces and august Egyptian faces, and now and again to name a divinity by the staff in his hand or by a bird fluttering over his head.[95]*

Each of the rose-petal gods and goddesses dance with a mortal who surrenders to the bliss of an alchemical sacred marriage, while Eros, the veiled God of Love, moves among them. Aherne also dances with one of these goddesses and is borne away in a mystic rapture – until he realises that he is about to be utterly subsumed by her, and that he will become merely a vessel for her to exist in the human realm. Too terrified to undergo this initiatory death, he awakens from the trance and flees in terror to the safety of the Catholic Church. He has exchanged the Rose for the rosary, which he now wears constantly around his neck in a wholesale retreat from the terrifying world of the Immortal Ones he had once longed to embrace.

The story echoes the ideas of Éliphas Lévi, the celebrated 19th century ceremonial magician who was a strong influence on Yeats' Rosicrucian views. In his *History of Magic* Lévi describes the Rose as expressing 'humanity aspiring to a natural religion, full of love and reason, founded on the revelation of the harmonies of existence of which the Rose was for initiates a living and blooming symbol... While religion toiled to prepare and establish the universal, exclusive, and definitive triumph of the Cross'. For Yeats, the reuniting of the Rose with the Cross would be an alchemical marriage which would transfigure not only the individual, but society and its religion as well.

Out of the Rose

Another story from The Secret Rose, titled, Out of the Rose, is set within a Christian Rosicrucian context, although this tale also has a melancholy, fin de siècle quality. It tells of an old knight who comes riding through the wooded slopes of Ben Bulben at sunset. The crest on his helmet is 'a small rose made of rubies that glimmered every moment to a deeper crimson'. Stretching his arms towards the west, he cries: 'O Divine Rose of Intellectual Flame, let the gates of thy peace be opened to me at last!'[96]

The knight tells how he is the last of the Knights of St. John and explains that the 'Rose of Rubies' on his crest is a symbol of his life and hope. He served under 'a knight of Palestine' to whom God himself had revealed the Truth:

*He had seen a great Rose of Fire, and a Voice out of the Rose
had told him how men would turn from the light of their own
hearts, and bow down before outer order and outer fixity, and
that then the light would cease . . . and that none of those who
had seen clearly the truth and the ancient way could enter into
the Kingdom of God, which is in the Heart of the Rose, if they
stayed on willingly in the corrupted world; and so they must prove
their anger against the Powers of Corruption by dying in the
service of the Rose of God. While the Knight of Palestine was
telling us these things we seemed to see in a vision a crimson Rose
spreading itself about him, so that he seemed to speak out of its
heart, and the air was filled with fragrance.[97]*

*The visionary knight appears to have been based on the
legend of Brother Christian Rosencreutz, who had also
lived in Palestine where he gained mystical knowledge,
as recounted in the Fama Fraternitatis. Yeats' Golden
Dawn training is also apparent here in the reference to
the Kingdom of God being in the heart of the Rose, like
the luminous white centre of the Rose-Cross lamen, which
represents the divine presence at the top of the Tree of Life.
The story ends with the knight's death which he welcomes,
since he will be reunited with the heavenly Rose of God.*

Yeats regarded his books as sacred objects that had a talismanic power. He wanted their cover designs to reflect as closely as possible the numinous quality of the words inside. In Dublin's occult circles, he discovered an artist who could do just this in the person of Althea Gyles, a young artist and poet who, like Yeats, was connected with the Theosophists and the Golden Dawn. Althea was 'very tall with dusky red-gold hair and a voice of commanding music…' Yeats called her art 'the personification of the beauty which cannot be seen with the bodily eyes or pictured otherwise than by symbols.' As a Symbolist, Althea used the Rose throughout her own work. Yeats featured her in an essay he wrote on Symbolic Art for the Dublin magazine, *The Dome*, in which he described her favourite drawing, *The Rose of God*, (which the editor considered too risqué to print):

> *…a naked woman whose hands outstretched against the clouds as upon a cross, in the traditional attitude of the bride, the symbol of the microcosm in the Kaballa; while two winds, two destinies, the one full of white, the other full of red rose petals, personifying all purities and all passions, while about her descend upon a fleet of ships and a walled city personifying the wavering and fixed powers, the masters of the world in the alchemical symbolism. Some imperfect but beautiful verses accompany the drawing and describe her as for 'living man's delight and his eternal revering when dead.'* [98]

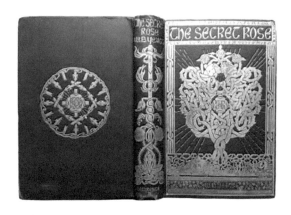

Althea Gyles' cover for Yeats' *The Secret Rose*, 1897

In 1897 he commissioned her to create the cover for *The Secret Rose*, and was delighted with the way her ornate, symbolic designs were such a perfect match for his theme.

The cover designs are in gilt-foil on dark blue cloth, the solar and lunar colours. The tree emerges from the skeleton of a dead knight, suggesting the spiritual rebirth that follows the death of the egoic self. It arises in a profusion of Celtic knotwork, reminiscent of a richly illustrated medieval book. In the centre of the tree is a four-petalled Rose upon a cross, perhaps symbolic of the four elements or the four worlds in Qabala. The Rose is at the position of Tiphareth on the Qabalistic tree. Tiphareth means Beauty, with the additional sense of Harmony. It stands on the Middle Pillar at the centre of the Tree of Life as a bridge between the material world below and the spiritual realm above. An initiate who reaches the level of Tiphareth sacrifices his or her ego-identity and becomes identified instead with the spiritual Self. The heavenly body associated with this sephirah is the Sun, hence the rays of golden light emanating from it. Above the Rose, two lovers emerge from the branches and kiss, each with a hand on the top of the cross. They have transcended the material world and are united in a *hieros gamos.* Above them are three roses in the position of the highest sephiroth on the Tree. Above the female lover on the left is Binah, the sephirah of the Mother, while above the male is Chokmah, the Father. This pair of primordial opposites are the two cosmic principles, (comparable to Shiva and Shakti in Hindu tradition) who give birth to the worlds of creation. The Rose at the top of the tree represents Kether, the Crown, the indivisible Divine.

On the back of the book is a circular mandala which perfectly captures the theme of *The Secret Rose*, which Yeats described as having 'but one subject, the war of the spiritual with the natural order'. The rose-cross in the centre of threatening spearheads perfectly illustrates the tension between these two realities – Heaven and Earth, eternity and death. The front and back covers of the book illustrate a passage from the story, *Rosa Alchemica*, in which the narrator is given a 'curiously wrought bronze box' in preparation for his initiation into the magical order:

> *In the box was a book bound in vellum, and having a rose-tree growing from an armed anatomy, and enclosing the faces of two lovers painted on the one side, to symbolise certainly the coming of beauty out of corruption, and probably much else; and upon the other the alchemical rose with many spears thrusting against it, but in vain, as was shown by the shattered points of those nearest to the petals. The book*

was written upon vellum, and in beautiful clear letters,
interspersed with symbolical pictures and illuminations,
after the manner of the Splendor Solis.[99]

For the reader of this original edition, decorated in such ornate and esoteric designs, the book described in *Rosa Alchemica* turns out to be the very book he or she is holding. This device clarifies Yeats' intention to create a book which was in itself a precious, talismanic object like the illuminated alchemical tome, *Splendor Solis.* Within its covers was a treasury of teachings on spiritual alchemy, which is defined in this story as 'the gradual distillation of the contents of the soul,' for those that 'were ready to put off the mortal and put on the immortal.' [100]

The spine of the book is no less extraordinary, showing a spear with its head dipping into a bowl or cauldron. It refers to an Irish myth of the magical spear of the God Lugh, which thirsted for blood and frequently burst into flames. It had to be kept submerged in a cauldron filled with a sleeping-draught of pounded poppy leaves. The spear in the cauldron also depicts sexual intercourse between male and female, suggesting this tale may have been a debased redaction of an earlier cosmological myth. Lugh is associated with the Sun and the lightning flash; the cauldron is a traditional image of the creation goddess. It reappears in the later stories of the Holy Grail where drops of blood flow from the tip of a deadly lance into the Grail itself. [101] At the top of the spear flames are bursting out, but lower down, poppies weave around it like a caduceus. The alchemical symbols for Fire and Water, as two triangles, can be seen on its hilt. Fire and Water, Sun and Moon, played an important part in Yeats' philosophy and

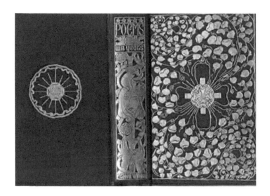

Althea Gyles' cover design for Yeats' *Poems*, 1899

poetry, and emphasize the union of opposites, which is the theme of all three remarkable illustrations.

Althea Gyles also created the cover art for the 1899 edition of Yeats' poetry, which continued to be used for the next thirty years.

The Rose at the centre of the cross is surrounded by a swirling cloud of petals, while spiralling lines emanate from its heart, suggesting, perhaps, its heavenly fragrance. On the spine, a pair of hands reach up imploringly to a woman whose eyes are raised heavenwards to the winged spirits of birds. She is surrounded by roses, and her distant expression suggests that she portrays the 'far-off, inviolable Rose' of Yeats' poem. Petals rain down on the hands, their shapes reminiscent of the divine sparks of heavenly light, sometimes called *yods,* in the Rider-Waite tarot deck that Yeats may have helped design. The back cover is graced by a simpler rose-cross mandala.

Yeats spent much of his youth in County Sligo, northwest Ireland, exploring the faery lore that inspired his early poetry. He collected folktales from the local country dwellers and was particularly interested in the High Faery race known as the *Sídhe,* (pronounced *shee*). Their name was originally *aes sídhe*, literally, 'the people who live in a mound,' and they had once been the ancient gods and goddesses of Ireland, known as the Tuatha Dé Danann, (the people of the goddess Danu). This noble race had once ruled on the surface of Ireland, but when they were defeated by an army of invaders, they were banished to live in palaces beneath the earth. In traditional Ireland it was believed that they were still there, living a secret life except at those 'thin' times of the year, particularly the Three Spirit Nights of Bealtaine, Midsummer and Samhain, when they ventured into the human world and became visible to those who have the gift of inner sight. Yeats found that, despite two thousand years of cultural repression by the Church, their complex and splendid mythology was still alive within the hearts and minds of the country people.

Yeats himself had his own vision of a procession of the *Sídhe*, that occurred spontaneously in 1898:

> *I closed my eyes a moment ago, and a company of people in blue robes swept by me in a blinding light, and had gone before I had done more than see little roses embroidered on the hems of their robes, and confused, blossoming apple-boughs somewhere beyond them, and recognised one of the company by his square, black, curling beard. I have often*

seen him; and one night a year ago I asked him questions which he answered by showing me flowers and precious stones, of whose meaning I had no knowledge, and he seemed too perfected a soul for any knowledge that cannot be spoken in symbol or metaphor.[102]

He wove an image from this vision into an early poem, *To Ireland in the Coming Times*:

> *... the red-rose-bordered hem*
> *Of her, whose history began*
> *Before God made the angelic clan,*
> *Trails all about the written page.*

Here the red-rose-bordered hem clearly belongs to the primordial goddess – perhaps Danu herself, although that is but one of her many names in Ireland.

Riders of the Sídhe by Scottish artist, John Duncan, 1911

Yeats' vision was in keeping with a long tradition of the rose being associated with an Otherwordly race. We have already noted this in the German legend of Tannhäuser, who visited the goddess in her Rose Garden within a mountain. As the rose was sacred to the Goddess, it stands to reason that it should also be sacred to the Faery Queen, who is an aspect of her. Her rose is the original wild variety, *rosa canina,* the 'dog rose', which has five green sepals and petals in a circle. Her other sacred flowers, apple-blossom and hawthorn, also have five petals apiece, and belong to the same family as the Rose.

Dog Rose and Hawthorn

In the Scottish ballad of Tam Lin, the heroine, Janet,
plucks a 'double rose' at the well of Carterhaugh and
attracts the attention of its guardian spirit, Tam Lin. Once
a human knight, this young man had been held in captivity
in the faery realm by its queen. Janet unwittingly summoned
him by picking his roses:

She had na pu'd a double rose,
A rose but only twa,
Till upon then started young Tam Lin,
Says, Lady, thou's pu nae mae.

Why pu's thou the rose, Janet,
And why breaks thou the wand?
Or why comes thou to Carterhaugh
Withouten my command?

Tam Lin had become the genus loci of the sacred well and
was angry that his roses had been picked by an intruder.
Yet, as the flower of love, the rose in this ballad is also a
prelude to the passion that grows between Janet and Tam
Lin.[103] The story of their love for each other culminates
in Janet's dramatic rescue of Tam Lin from the Queen of
Fairies who would keep him for herself. This archaic tale
encodes the ancient tension between the mortal human race
and the immortal faery race, as symbolised by the two roses.

Painting by Scottish artist, Herbert McNair,
based on the story of Tamlaine (Tam Lin), 1905.

Another story of the faery rose takes place in the heart of the south Tyrolean mountains which was once home to a race of dwarves. Their king, Laurin, had a magnificent rose-garden, but sadly, it was destroyed by evil human invaders. Yet still, at dawn and dusk, the mountains glow with a soft pink light, a reminder of the beauty that once grew there.

MEDITATION VII –
THE ROSE-BORDERED HEM

*The following meditation is based on Yeats' vision of
the Sídhe, the ancient gods and goddesses of Ireland.
It is set in a place known as The Glen in County
Sligo, northwest Ireland, where Yeats spent much of
his youth exploring the faery lore that inspired his
early poetry. His poem, The Hosting of the Sídhe,
describes how the faeries gather in The Glen before
riding up to the sacred hill of Knocknarea, (the Hill
of the Queen) on the three Spirit Nights of the year.*

Take a few deep breaths and relax completely...

You are sitting in the wooded glen below
Knocknarea on the eve of Bealtaine, with your back
against the rough bark of a twisted hawthorn tree.
The steep, rocky walls on either side are covered
with emerald green ferns and draped with hanging
curtains of ivy. As you inhale the strange, musky
scent of the hawthorn blossoms and listen to the soft
hypnotic trickling of little waterfalls, you are lulled
into a dreamy state of mind in which you are not
quite awake and not quite asleep . . .

Now you become dimly aware of another sound
– the gentle rhythmic jangling of a horse's bridle.
You gaze in wonder as a white horse, caparisoned
in burnished gold, comes into view down the glen.

The rider is a tall and beautiful Lady wearing an iridescent white gown with little red and white roses interwoven through the hem. The crown of white May blossom on her head identifies her as Niamh, the leader of the host that rides between the worlds on this magical eve. In the glimmering twilight, you can make out the Riders of the Sídhe following in her train: beautiful lords and ladies with pale faces, arrayed in rich robes of sapphire and carmine, amber and ivory, each bearing a silver star upon the brow.

She is about to ride past you, seemingly into the rock itself. But mesmerised by the extraordinary procession and the beauty of the Lady, you leap to your feet and call out to her to stay a moment. . . She wheels her horse around and looks at you, throwing back her head with a silvery laugh, and although she does not appear to speak in the usual way, you hear her say:

Come with me, come with me: I will make you immortal! I am the sunlight in the heart, the moonlight in the mind; I am the light at the end of every dream, the voice for ever calling to come away; I am the desire beyond joy or tears. for my palace opens into the Gardens of the Sun, and there are the fire-fountains which quench the heart's desire in rapture.

She begins to sing of Tír na nÓg, the Land of the Ever-Living, and your heart swells with the longing to follow her to where there is no pain and no death, no sorrow and no mourning, but only life and light and beauty beyond earthly imagination. The hosting faeries surround you and eager hands reach out to help you up onto her horse. Then the Queen wheels around to face the hill, and gives a strange high call, whereupon a great pair of golden gates appear in the rock.

As the gates noiselessly glide open, you become aware that the Host is singing in high chanting voices:

The great gates of the mountain are open once again,
And the sound of song and dancing falls upon the ears
of men,
The Land of youth lies gleaming, touched with rainbow
light and mirth,
And the old enchantment lingers in the honey-heart of
Earth.

And now you are galloping away into the mountain, followed by the hosts of the Sídhe like a great wind, and when the last of the riders is through, the gates close behind you, then vanish completely.

You are riding over a vast plain of emerald green, surrounded by a ring of opalescent mountains.

Everything is illumined by a pure and liquid light – a living light that comes not from Sun or Moon, but from a glowing star far above in a sky the colour of pearl. The light has a voice and its music hangs glittering in the air like starlight. In no time at all you have arrived in the heart of this land: a city of cloud palaces, seemingly made of shifting rainbow light, in the midst of which is an enormous shining Tree of Life, whose roots can be seen growing down through the transparent earth into unfathomable depths, while its branches soar up to the sky, its crown lost in the stars. This is the Tree that joins all the worlds, above and below, and within it you can see the heavenly influences streaming down from the stars to meet the forces of the Earth which rise up out of the deep, in a continual exchange of pure life energy: a process of infinite regeneration. Its branches spread as far as the eye can see in all directions, sending out this force into this Otherworld, and thence out into our own, where it becomes the etheric foundation of all physical life.

But now your attention is drawn away from the Tree by the sound of high, silvery voices singing and playing on musical instruments, the beauty of which you have never heard before. The Queen is calling you to join a dance, and the next moment you are whirling and spinning around in joyous, ecstatic motion, light as a leaf, or bird of the air... The starry faces of the Sídhe swirl about you, and as you dance with now one, now another, you learn many things about this wondrous land that is only a breath away from our own...

And now you are being led towards a sumptuous feast laid out in a banqueting hall, where the tables are piled high with bowls of fruit, nuts, aromatic sweetmeats and crystal flagons of sparkling wines. But you hesitate, remembering the old warning that to eat of faery food means you will never return to your earthly home.

As you draw back, you hear a soft rustling sigh like the wind in trees around the hall, and you realise your time in the Land of Light is coming to an end, for you have not the willingness to stay here forever. One of the Sídhe leads you behind the great Tree, where you see a little door you had not noticed before. The moment you step through, you find yourself pushing through a hanging curtain of ivy, and now you are back in The Glen where all is silent and still in the twilight, except for the trickle of water. The door has disappeared, and you wonder if perhaps you had fallen asleep and dreamt everything... but then at your feet you see a small rose, fallen from the hem of a gown.

Gently picking up the rose, you make your way out of the Glen down a muddy path as night begins to fall. As you reach the road, you are startled to see the little blossom change its shape before your eyes, and it now looks like something quite different. An inner knowing tells you this is a key that will enable you to enter the gates of Faerie at a future time. But for now you are ready to return to the simple joys and loves of your earthly life . . . Yawn and stretch and become aware of your body sitting in your room again. When you are ready, open your eyes and come fully back to present time. Write down your thoughts and feelings from this experience.

CHAPTER EIGHT

THE ROSE AND THE FIRE

Marvel!
a garden among the flames!
– Ibn 'Arabi

ROSE OF MEMORY

s we now turn to a later age, the question must be asked: Can this flower of divine beauty and wisdom, that has imbued past ages and cultures with such rich significance, still blossom in the wastelands of the post-modern world? One who speaks for the timeless message of the Rose is the celebrated poet, T.S. Eliot. Although he wrote in the 20th century, his vision of the Rose as a salvific image continues to resonate with deep meaning and significance into current times.

Eliot looked to Dante as his poetic master, and his perception of the Rose is drawn from Dante's celestial vision in *Paradiso*. For example, in his poem, *The Hollow Men*, a desolate lament about the moral and spiritual bankruptcy of modern humanity, Eliot contrasts the godless lives of the 'hollow men' with the beatific souls of the 'multifoliate rose' who live in the light of divine love. The chilling sense of despair in this poem, written in 1925, was born out of the horrors of the First World War and its aftermath, which had also prompted Eliot's famous poem, *The Waste Land.* He was also deeply unhappy in his personal life, where it was clear to him that his marriage to Vivienne Haigh-Wood was a failure. The unbearable nihilism expressed in *The Hollow Men* was transformed when, two years later, he converted to the Anglican church. Among the first fruits of his conversion was the poem *Ash Wednesday,* which is filled with liturgical rhythms, biblical phrases and allusions to the *Divina Commedia.* Here the Rose is associated with a divine feminine figure addressed as both 'Lady' and 'Mother' in lines reminiscent of mediaeval Marian poetry:

> *Lady of silences*
> *Calm and distressed*
> *Torn and most whole*
> *Rose of memory*
>
> *Rose of forgetfulness*
> *Exhausted and life-giving*
> *Worried reposeful*
> *The single Rose*
> *Is now the Garden*
> *Where all loves end*
>   *...*
> *Grace to the Mother*
> *For the Garden*
> *Where all love ends.*[104]

Although she is clearly to be identified as the Virgin Mary, the lines, 'Rose of memory / Rose of forgetfulness' also recall how Dante forgot Beatrice after she died and fell into sinful ways. Yet in time his love for her reawakened and was transformed into the highest spiritual love in the Earthly Paradise. These lines may represent Eliot's desire to sublimate his unhappy experience in relationship with an actual woman to a transcendent love for the divine feminine. He thanks 'the Mother' for 'the Garden / Where all love ends,' for it signifies the end of difficult worldly relationships and the entry into Paradise, the place where eternal Love resides.

FOUR QUARTETS

But it is in Eliot's brilliant philosophical meditation on time and eternity, *Four Quartets,* that the Rose blossoms into the image of divine beauty and wisdom as understood in previous ages. It becomes one of the most important themes in this sequence of poems, starting with the first, *Burnt Norton,* where he catches a glimpse of the eternal bliss that miraculously intersects the world of time. Unlike Yeats with his Rosicrucian background, Eliot does not use the image of the rose upon the cross, and yet it's possible to detect a trace of this potent symbol hidden in the very structure of the poems. Designed to suggest movements of a musical quartet, each of the four poems is based upon one of the four elements of the physical world. The main theme of the sequence is Eliot's attempts to reconcile the world of time with the timeless world of spirit, the 'still point' at the centre of the turning world, which, as we have seen, the Rosicrucians expressed as the rose at the centre of a four-armed cross.

Each poem is set in a different place that had deep personal meaning for the poet. The first, *Burnt Norton*, takes its name from a manor house in the Cotswolds, England, which had been burnt down by its mad owner in the 18th century. In September 1934, Eliot, now separated from his wife, was out walking with his long-time friend, Emily Hale, when they accidentally wandered into its semi-wild rose garden. In the neglected, yet still beautiful garden, Eliot experienced an unforgettable, timeless moment which inspired the poem he was to write one year later.

The Unopened Door

*The rose garden is both an actual place in the Cotswolds
and a symbol of paradise, the lost Eden from which we
have been exiled and to which we long to return. For Eliot,
the rose-garden was also 'the first world' of childhood
with its innocent joys, filled with the presence of invisible
children: 'Hidden excitedly, containing laughter'. It is also
a place of 'what might have been' – of regrets for lost
opportunities for happiness that never came to fruition.*

*Footfalls echo in the memory
Down the passage which we did not take
Towards the door we never opened
Into the rose-garden.* – T. S. Eliot[105]

The general air of neglect and decay in the garden is also a metaphor for Eliot's own psyche at this time. Although the opening of *Burnt Norton* has universal significance, it can also be read on a personal level as an expression of Eliot's grief for his failed marriage and lack of children. At this time, Vivienne had been committed to a mental hospital, and Eliot's religious beliefs prevented him from pursuing a divorce from her. When he joined the Anglican Church, he had taken a vow of celibacy.

Several people who knew them well believed that Eliot was in love with Emily Hale, a friend from his student days in Harvard. The consensus was they might have married had not Vivienne been still alive. It's significant that the experience in the rose garden took place in 'autumn heat': Although Eliot was only forty-six years old at this time, he felt he had long passed the summer of his youth, yet this and other allusions in the poem clearly carry a suggestion of sexual passion in later life. There is also an implication that something more may have taken place between Eliot and Emily in the garden, according to a Boston friend of the poet, who added that 'the few who knew what happened there were sworn to secrecy and are now dead.'[106]

Long after the experience in the rose-garden and Vivienne's death, Eliot did finally find fulfilment in his second marriage to his young secretary, Valerie Fletcher. In *A Dedication to my Wife* written in 1956, the year after they married, he wrote of their happiness now that they had entered and taken possession of the rose garden, which here is very much a place of earthly joys:

No peevish winter wind shall chill
No sullen tropic sun shall wither
The roses in the rose-garden which is ours and ours only.[107]

THE GARDEN BEYOND TIME

In the opening lines of *Burnt Norton,* he expresses a sense of futility at hankering after the unattainable, since the past cannot be altered:

...to what purpose
Disturbing the dust on a bowl of rose-leaves
I do not know.[108]

But Eliot goes deeper: the rose is seen not only as a symbol of mortal love in the temporal world, but also the heavenly blossom of the infinite Love that transcends time and death. In *Burnt Norton*, the passage that leads from the time-bound sphere is opened by a bird that calls him to step through 'the first gate'. Like the rose garden itself, the bird in this poem was most likely both a real thrush Eliot heard and also, like birds in all mythological traditions, a messenger from the spirit world. (As well as its melodious song, thrushes do in fact make urgent-sounding calls that could be interpreted as 'Quick!' and 'Go, go, go'). This passage has something of the delight of children's stories in which everyday life is suddenly transformed into the magical: Alice steps through the looking glass, a wardrobe leads to Narnia. Perhaps most of all it recalls *The Secret Garden*, the book written by Francis Hodgson Burnett in 1911, where the unhappy child follows the song of a robin into a beautiful hidden garden that transforms her world. Eliot is aware that the summons of the thrush is illusory, a 'deception', yet is willing to suspend his belief in linear time to enter into a magical world where time does not exist.

The invisible inhabitants of the garden – the children, or possibly, Adam and Eve, – lead the poet to one of three dry concrete pools in the grounds, where he has an epiphany, a sublime moment in which he catches a glimpse of eternity, and Paradise is found.

> *And the pool was filled with water out of sunlight,*
> *And the lotos rose, quietly, quietly,*
> *The surface glittered out of heart of light,*
> *And they were behind us, reflected in the pool.*[109]

Although everything in the poet's world is 'dry' and 'drained', and the garden is full of withered autumn leaves, sunlight floods the pool with light, giving the illusion of shining water, through which a lotus blossom silently arises. In Hindu and Buddhist traditions (with which Eliot was familiar) the lotus symbolises eternity, purity, divinity, and is widely used to denote life, fertility, and renewal. It is also described as growing within the human subtle energy system: The lotus roots itself in mud – the unregenerate self – but through specific yogic practices, appears to grow up the spine to reach the crown chakra at the top of the head, where it opens into a thousand-petalled lotus blossom. Known as the Door to Brahman and the Source of Light, it gives rise to a sublime experience of divine consciousness. Behind the poet's reflection in the pool, he can see the invisible beings of the garden, implying that

165

from the perspective of the Eternal, time does not exist. Yet Eliot's epiphany is fleeting: 'a cloud passed, and the pool was empty'. As he says in an oft-quoted line, 'humankind / Cannot bear very much reality', in recognition that this experience, far from being an illusion, is the essentially Real, the timeless ground of being that underlies the time-bound world of appearances, an experience too overwhelming for the human mind to tolerate for long.

At the end of this section and the whole movement, Eliot concludes that it is only through the finite that we can apprehend the Infinite, the experience in the rose garden, because the Eternal is immanent in the present moment of time. If we can achieve that special state of heightened 'rose garden' consciousness, we can move from existence to essence; from the actual to the real. The nature of the paradox is that 'Only through time time is conquered'. We can only get a glimpse of eternity by entering fully into time, by taking the journey into the rose garden where time and eternity intersect.

Lotus in bloom within a pool

In the subsequent three poems of *Four Quartets*, the Rose becomes entwined with another major symbol: Fire, which burns through the verses with the intensity of destruction, purification, illumination, and, finally, of divine love itself.[110] The fire of destruction is both within and without: the raging fever of worldly passions within the human ego and its worst outer expression: the hellfire of war. In the fourth poem, *Little Gidding,* written at the height of World War II, Eliot imagines himself walking by night through the desolate, burnt-out streets of London during the Blitz, where he served as an air raid warden. In this poem, Time annihilates life and there is no rebirth. The roses from the magical garden of *Burnt Norton* have been reduced to ashes:

> *Ash on an old man's sleeve*
> *Is all the ash the burnt roses leave.*[111]

The only way out of this modern inferno, is paradoxically through committing oneself to the flames of purification as Dante did in his *Purgatorio*:

> *If to be warmed, then I must freeze*
> *and quake in purgatorial fires,*
> *Of which the flame is roses, and the smoke is briars.*[112]

The fires of Purgatory freeze and burn away our deepest longings and desires, yet they are fuelled by the briars and blossoms of the Rose, which, as the poem progresses, becomes increasingly understood as a symbol of Divine

Love. As the alchemist, Paracelsus, said: 'You should understand that alchemy is nothing but the art which makes the impure into the pure through fire.'

The pain and heartbreak we experience through a life catastrophe such as losing one dear to us, or enduring a terrible accident or disease, plummets our whole being into what seems like a purgatory of endless suffering. The person we once thought ourselves to be, and the familiar, comfortable life we once lived, is burned away by flames of torment. Yet:

> *Who then devised the torment? Love.*
> *Love is the unfamiliar Name*
> *Behind the hands that wove*
> *The intolerable shirt of flame*
> *Which human power cannot remove.*
> *We only live, only suspire*
> *Consumed by either fire or fire.* [113]

Eliot is saying that we can either succumb to living as if we were only the personality housed in a perishable body with all its burning desires for ego gratification, and suffer the disappointments, losses and pain that life inevitably brings due to its constantly changing and impermanent nature and die in despair and ignorance. . . or we can choose to go consciously through the 'baptism of fire' that life puts us through and emerge from the pyre as a new Self, rooted in the unchanging world of Spirit that underlies this world of appearances and filled with the inner knowing that the whole experience has been orchestrated by Divine Love.

Eliot's poetic resolution of the Fire and the Rose was inspired by
Dante Alighieri, whose supreme vision of Paradise is figured as a
Rose ablaze with the radiant presence of ascended
souls and heavenly beings of Light.
(Illustration from the original by Gustave Doré).

The poem arrives at its triumphant climax in which the
tyranny of Time is conquered and all opposites are reconciled.

> *We shall not cease from exploration*
> *And the end of all our exploring*
> *Will be to arrive where we started*
> *And know the place for the first time.*
> *Through the unknown, remembered gate*
> *When the last of earth left to discover*
> *Is that which was the beginning;*
> *At the source of the longest river*
> *The voice of the hidden waterfall*
> *And the children in the apple-tree*
> *Not known, because not looked for*
> *But heard, half-heard, in the stillness*
> *Between two waves of the sea.*
> *Quick now, here, now, always –*
> *A condition of complete simplicity*
> *(Costing not less than everything)*
> *And all shall be well and*
> *All manner of thing shall be well*
> *When the tongues of flame are in-folded*
> *Into the crowned knot of fire*
> *And the fire and the rose are one.*[114]

As in *Ash Wednesday*, Love is the great resolver of all
paradoxes. Now we can return to the longed-for rose
garden, for the gate is open wide; in fact, we now see it was
never closed, except to our clouded perception. When we
give up our search for happiness in the past and future, and
enter into the holiness of the present moment, we realise

that what we seek has always been, and will always be 'here, now, always'. But our liberation can only come when we are willing to surrender the totality of who we think we are, and submit to the redemptive, purifying fire of Divine Love.

Then, even in this imperfect, war-torn world, comes the miracle: Quoting from the mystical visions of the 14th century anchorite, Julian of Norwich, collected in her book, *Revelations of Divine Love,* hope dawns for a transfigured future when 'All manner of thing shall be well'.

The flames of Hell and Purgatory are transformed into the brilliant fire of the Holy Spirit, as in Dante's vision of the celestial white rose, and the 'tongues of flame' which descended upon the apostles of Christ at the Pentecost. The Rose, Time's loveliest flower, is shot through with the glory of the Infinite: heaven and earth indivisible.

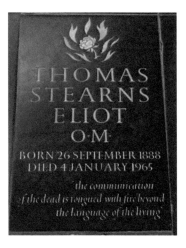

At Poets' Corner in Westminster Abbey, T. S. Eliot is commemorated with a memorial stone depicting a rose surrounded by flames.

The rambling journey of the Rose has taken us a long way from the innocent and joyful world of the goddesses of antiquity. From there we explored the many ways in which the Western psyche has sought to balance body and soul, Heaven and Earth, the red rose and the white in its endless search for reconnection with the Source. Yet, even in this degenerate age of rapacious materialism, Eliot's genius leads us to a new understanding of its incorruptible purity and power. Rising from the dust and ashes of a world addicted to war and destruction, the Rose is revealed as an imperishable vision of timeless beauty and love, a Chalice of Light that nourishes and sustains the human soul. Its fragrance comes to us from a higher reality: a Brighter World that both lies beyond the physical dimension yet intersects it at every point so that the transcendent is fully alive and present within every single particle of the immanent. And the Mystic Rose also blooms within the individual soul, that, pierced by the thorns of experience, may now unfurl to receive the blissful Light of the Divine.

MEDITATION VIII –
THE FIRE OF ROSES

This final meditation is based on a passage from one of my favourite children's books: The Princess and Curdie, by George MacDonald, the 19th century author who was such an inspiration to C.S. Lewis. I have always been fascinated by the fire of roses and its message of purification and redemption through the sacrificial flames of Love.

Close your eyes and take a few deep breaths. You are walking through a quiet, dim wood in a dusky autumn twilight. Feel and hear the crackle of fallen leaves underfoot and inhale the earthy smell of damp earth and trees. After a while, you arrive at a clearing to see a strange sight. In the centre is a blazing, crackling fire on which an old peasant woman is heaping whole rose blossoms and rose petals. The flames burn pink and gold and emit an intoxicating fragrance . . .

You cannot go farther: this is the Fire of Roses, the sacrificial fire that purifies the heart and mind of dross. There is only one way to go, for this is a Fire of Purification through which you must pass. You approach the flames, and the woman looks at you with ancient, wise and loving eyes. Step into the flames. Although the fierce pain may take your breath away, you remain steadfast of purpose. The roaring furnace of flame now completely surrounds you.

Then above the crackle of the flames, you hear a new sound – the Lady of the Rose-Fire is weeping because of your pain and all that you have ever suffered in your life or many lives, for she is the Mother of the World, and there is not one whose pain she does not feel as if it were the sorrow of her own child.

Now from within you, as if drawn out by the excruciating heat, appears a procession of images, memories and feelings of all that you have deeply suffered in this lifetime, past and present. Focus on each of these in turn and let yourself feel each one until you are ready to fully let go of it with total equanimity and, if relevant, forgiveness for wrongs done to you... Each one is consumed by the flames and floats up as smoke, finally disappearing into the air. . .

When no more impressions are generated, you feel two hands firmly clasping your own. You look down and the old woman's cool, surprisingly smooth hands lead you out of the flames to the other side.

Here, you find yourself in a Rose Garden. The Old Woman has become a tall and beautiful Lady who leads you to the heart of the garden, where an arbour of roses encircles a fountain of clear, shining water that flows out into the four directions . . . Here you may bathe and cool yourself in the sparkling, revivifying shower. When you emerge refreshed from the cleansing water, you feel lighter and freer than when you first set forth on this journey.

The Lady now plucks a sprig of roses, one red and one white, and offers it to you. As you take it in your hand, the garden vanishes. You rise up out of your body into the heavens. Above you in the sky glows a pure white rose, *Rosa Mystica*. Below you on the Earth, glows the deep red rose, *Rosa Mundi*. You see that you are in between these two roses, contained within a rose of pink and burnished gold like a living fire. Each petal is a flame of lambent light. You are suffused with the glowing opalescent light of the Rose of Fire, *Rosa Igni*. But in *this* fire there is no pain, for you have been purified within and without . . . . Stay within this place until it is time for you to return. Then gently open your eyes and come all the way back. Write down your thoughts and feelings from this experience.

BIBLIOGRAPHY

Apuleius, *The Isis-book, (Metamorphoses, Book XI)*, (Leiden: Brill Archive, 1975)

Baring, Anne, and Jules Cashford, *The Myth of the Goddess: Evolution of an Image*, (London: Penguin UK, 1993)

Bazin, Germain, *Paradeisos, The Art of the Garden,* (Boston: Little, Brown and Co, 1990)

Benko, Stephen, *The Virgin Goddess: Studies in the Pagan and Christian Roots of Mariology*, (Leiden: Brill, 2004)

Bindon, Peter, *The Secret Rosicrucian Tradition*, (New York: AMORC, 2004)

Brookes, John, *Gardens of Paradise,* (London: Weidenfeld and Nicolson, 1987)

Burckhardt, Titus, *Alchemy: Science of the Cosmos, Science of the Soul*, (Shaftesbury: Element Books 1986)

Burckhardt, Titus, *Chartres and the Birth of the Cathedral*, Bloomington: (Indiana, World Wisdom Books, 2010)

Chevalier, Jean, and Alain Gheerbrant, *A Dictionary of Symbols*, (New York: Penguin Group USA, 1996)

Churton, Tobias, *Invisibles: The True History of the Rosicrucians*, (Addlestone: Lewis Masonic Pub., 2011)

Cirlot, J. E. *A Dictionary of Symbols,* (Dorchester: Dorset Press, 1994)

Clark, Emma, *The Art of the Islamic Garden*, (Marlborough; Crowood Press, 2011)

Cooper, J.C., *An Illustrated Encyclopaedia of Traditional Symbols*, (London: Thames & Hudson, 1987)

Cowen, Painton, *The Rose Window: Splendour and Symbol*, (New York: Thames & Hudson, 2005)

Critchlow, Keith, (*The Hidden Geometry of Flowers: Living Rhythms, Form and Number*, (Edinburgh: Floris Books, 2011)

De Cleene, Marcel and Lejeune, Marie C., *Compendium of Symbolic and Ritual Plants in Europe: Trees and shrubs*, (Ghent, Belgium: Man and Culture Publishers, 2002)

De Lorris, Guillaume, and D. Meun, Jean, *The Romance of the Rose*, (Princeton: Princeton University Press, 1995)

Drew, Elizabeth A, *T.S. Eliot, the Design of His Poetry*, (Oxfordshire: Taylor & Francis, 1950)

Durling, Robert M., *The Divine Comedy of Dante Alighieri: Volume 3: Paradiso*, (Oxford: Oxford University Press, 2010)

Eliade, Mircea, *The Encyclopedia of Religion,* (New York: Macmillan, 1987)

Eliot, T.S. *Four Quartets,* (London: Faber and Faber, 1970)

Eliot, T.S. *Collected Poems 1909-1962,* (London: Faber and Faber, 1979)

Ellmann, Richard, *Yeats, The Man and the Masks*, (New York: W.W. Norton & Co., 1978)

Emre, Yunus, ed./trans. Kabir Helminski and Refik Algan, *The Drop that Became the Sea: Lyric Poems of Yunus Emre*, (Boulder, Co.: Shambhala Publications, 1989)

Freeman, Mara, *Grail Alchemy: Initiation in the Celtic Mystery Tradition*, (Rochester, Vermont: Destiny Books, 2014)

Gadon, Elinor W., *The Once and Future Goddess: A Symbol for Our Time*, (San Francisco: Harper San Francisco, 1990)

Godwin, Joscelyn, *The Chemical Wedding of Christian Rosenkreutz*, (Maine: Red Wheel/Weiser, 1991)

Goody, Jack, *The Culture of Flowers*, (Cambridge: Cambridge University Press, 1994)

Gordon, Lyndall, *T.S. Eliot: An Imperfect Life*, (New York: W.W. Norton & Co., 2000)

Gorski, William T., *Yeats and Alchemy*, (Albany: SUNY Press, 1996)

Graf, Susan J., *W. B. Yeats – Twentieth-century Magus*, (Maine: Weiser Books, 2000)

Green, Arthur, *The Heart of the Matter: Studies in Jewish Mysticism and Theology*, (Lincoln: University of Nebraska Press, 2015)

Grossman, Allan, *Poetic Knowledge in the Early Yeats*, (Charlottesville: University Press of Virginia, 1969)

Guénon, René, *The Esoterism of Dante*, (Hillsdale, NY: Sophia Perennis, 2004)

Guénon, René, Fohr, Henry D. and Fohr, Samuel D., *Symbols of Sacred Science*, (Hillsdale, NY: Sophia Perennis, 2004)

Hall, James, *Dictionary of Subjects and Symbols in Art*, (London: Routledge, 2018)

Harkness, Peter, *The Rose: An Illustrated History*, (Richmond Hill: Firefly Books, 2003)

Harper, George Mills, *Yeats' Golden Dawn,* (London: Macmillan, 1974)

Harvey, Andrew, *Teachings of Rumi*, (Boulder, Co.: Shambhala Publications, 1999)

Hesiod, *Theogony and Works and Days*, (Oxford: Oxford University Press, 1999)

Hobhouse, Penelope, *Gardens of Persia,* (London: Cassell Illustrated, 2006)

Huffman, William H., *Robert Fludd*, (Berkeley: North Atlantic Books, 2001)

Hutton, Frankie, *Rose Lore*, (Maryland: Lexington Books, 2015)

Jeffares, A. N., *A New Commentary on the Poems of W.B. Yeats*, (London: Palgrave Macmillan, 1984)

Jeffares, A. N., *W.B Yeats: A New Biography*, (London: Bloomsbury Publishing, 2001)

Khan, Inayat, *The Sufi Message of Hazrat Inayat Khan*, (New Lebanon, New York: Sufi Order Publications, 1982)

Khansari et al, *The Persian Garden: Echoes of Paradise,* (Washington, DC: Mage Publishers, 2004)

179

Kiaer, Eigil, *Methuen Handbook of Roses*, (London: Methuen & Co, 1953)

Krüssmann, Gerd, *The Complete Book of Roses*, (Oregon: Timber Press, 1981)

Lehner, Ernst and Johanna, *Folklore and Symbolism of Flowers, Plants and Trees*, (New York: Tudor Publishing Company, 1960)

Madauros, Apuleius O., *The Isis-Book (Metamorphoses, Book XI) ed/trans. by J. Gwyn Griffiths*, (Leiden: BRILL, 1975)

Matthews, John, et al, *The Rosicrucian Enlightenment Revisited*, (Hudson, NY: Steiner Books, 1999)

McIntosh, Christopher, *The Rosicrucians: The History, Mythology, and Rituals of an Esoteric Order*, (Maine: Weiser Books, 1998)

McIntosh, Christopher, *The Rosy Cross Unveiled: The History, Mythology and Rituals of an Occult Order*, (Maine, Weiser, 1997)

McLean, Adam, *The Alchemical Mandala: A Survey of the Mandala in the Western Esoteric Traditions*, (Maine: Red Wheel/Weiser, 2002)

McLean, Teresa, *Medieval English Gardens*, (North Chelmsford: Courier Corporation, 2014)

Moore, Virginia, *The Unicorn, William Butler Yeats' Search for Reality,* (New York: Macmillan Co., 1954)

Paterson, Allen, *A History of the Fragrant Rose*, (London: Little Books, 2006)

Putzel, Steven, *Reconstructing Yeats: The Secret Rose and The Wind Among the Reeds*, (Lanham: Rowman & Littlefield, 1986)

Raine, Kathleen, *Yeats the Initiate: Essays on Certain Themes in the Work of W.B. Yeats*, (Lanham: Rowman & Littlefield, 1990)

Roob, Alexander, *Alchemy and Mysticism,* (Köln: Taschen, 2016)

Rosenzweig, Rachel, *Worshipping Aphrodite: Art and Cult in Classical Athens*, Ann Arbor: University of Michigan Press, 2004)

Ruggles, D. Fairchild, *Gardens, Landscape, and Vision in the Palaces of Islamic Spain,* (University Park, Pennsylvania: The Pennsylvania State University Press, 2006)

Rumi, Jelaluddin, *Call to Love: In the Rose Garden with Rumi*, ed. by Andrew Harvey, (New York: Sterling Publishing Company, 2007)

Seward, Barbara, *The Symbolic Rose*, (New York: Columbia University Press, 1953)

Schimmel, Anne-Marie, *The Islamic Garden*, (Washington D.C.: Dumbarton Oaks, Trustees for Harvard University, 1976)

Shah, Idries, *The Sufis*, (London: Octagon Press, 1999)

Taylor, Brian William, *Gardens of the Gods*, (Shropshire: Clun Valley Publications, 1996)

Tergit, Gabriele, *Flowers Through the Ages*, (London: Charles Skilton, 1961)

Unterecker, John E., *A Reader's Guide to William Butler Yeats*, (New York: Syracuse University Press, 1959)

Waite, Arthur E., *Rosicrucian Rites and Ceremonies of the Fellowship of the Rosy Cross,* (Burnaby, BC, Canada: Ishtar Pub., 2008)

Waite, Arthur E., *The Brotherhood of the Rosy Cross*, (New York: University Books, 1924)

Waite, Arthur E., *The Pictorial Key to the Tarot*, (New York: University Books, 1966)

Waite, Arthur E., *The Real History of the Rosicrucians*, (New York: J. W. Bouton, 1900)

Wilkins, Eithne, *The Rose-garden Game: A Tradition of Beads and Flowers*, (London: Gollancz, 1969)

Winston-Allen, Anne, *Stories of the Rose: The Making of the Rosary in the Middle Ages*, (University Park: Penn State Press, 2010)

Yeats, W. B., *Letters; ed. by Allan Wade*, (New York: Macmillan, 1955)

Yeats, W. B., *Essays and Introductions*, (London: The Macmillan Press, 1974)

Yeats, William B., *Mythologies*, (London: Macmillan Press, 1959)

Yeats, William B., ed. by Peter Allt and Russell Alspach, *The Variorum Edition of the Poems of WB Yeats,* (New York: Macmillan, 1957)

Zuylen, Gabrielle V., *The Garden: Visions of Paradise*, (London: Thames & Hudson, 1995)

ENDNOTES

1   Quoted in Anne Baring and Jules Cashford, *The Myth of the Goddess*, (London: Penguin UK, 1993), p. 352.

2   Hesiod, *Theogony and Works and Days*, (New York: Oxford University Press, USA, 1999), pp. 199-212.

3   Rachel Rosenzweig, *Worshipping Aphrodite: Art and Cult in Classical Athens*, (Ann Arbor: University of Michigan Press, 2004), p. 29.

4   Ovid, *Fasti*, v.194-195.

5   Jack Goody, *The Culture of Flowers*, (Cambridge: Cambridge University Press, 1993), p. 41.

6   See: Apuleius O. Madauros, *The Isis-Book, (Metamorphoses, Book XI)*, ed./trans. by J. Gwyn Griffiths (Leiden: BRILL, 1975).

7   Percy E. Newberry, *On the Vegetable Remains discovered in the Cemetery of Hawara* in W. M. Flinders Petrie, *Hawara, Biahmu, and Arsinoe*, (London: Field & Tuer, 1889), p. 48.

8   Eithne Wilkins, *The Rose-garden Game: A Tradition of Beads and Flowers*, (London: Victor Gollancz, 1969), p. 144

9   Goody, p. 89.

10 From Marcel de Cleene and Mary Claire Lejeune, *Compendium of Symbolic and Ritual Plants in Europe*, (Ghent: Man and Culture Publishers, Belgium, 2003).

11 Anne Winston-Allen, *Stories of the Rose: The Making of the Rosary in the Middle Ages*, (University Park: Penn State Press, 2010), p. 98.

12 Winston-Allen, p. 104.

13 See: Elinor W. Gadon, *The Once and Future Goddess: A Symbol for Our Time*, (San Francisco: Harper San Francisco, 1990).

14 Stephen Benko, *The Virgin Goddess: Studies in the Pagan and Christian Roots of Mariology*, (Leiden: BRILL, 2004), p. 15.

15 Gabriele Tergit, *Flowers Through the Ages*, (Cornell: Cornell University, 1961), p. 43.

16 Wilkins, p. 117.

17 Wilkins, p. 117.

18 Edith Rickert, *Ancient English Christmas Carols*, (London: Chatto & Windus, 1928), p.8.f

19 From Cornelius van Sneek, *Sermones XXI super Confraternitate de Rosaceo*, Paris 1514. Quoted in: Wilkins, p. 113.

20 Teresa McLean, *Medieval English Gardens*, (North Chelmsford: Courier Corporation, 2014), p. 130.

21 In recent times there has been a popular revival of this practice, pioneered by the Mary's Gardens movement, which has discovered that historically some five hundred plants have been considered 'Flowers of Our Lady'. An enclosed garden provides a *temenos*, a secret place of the soul, a sanctuary for quiet contemplation. The trees act as a reminder of the Tree of Life, joining heaven and earth, while the flowers exemplify Mary's holy virtues that the devotee can emulate. Mary Gardens honour the aspect of Mary as 'Mother of All Growing Things', reminding us that *mater* and *matter* are one and the same. Catholic Christians and others who participate in this movement feel that the ritual of cultivating the soil of a Mary garden helps them develop an awareness of her living presence in the garden of their soul.

22 Samuel Noah Kramer, *The Biblical Song of Songs and the Sumerian Love Songs*, 2016 http://www.penn.museum/sites/expedition/?p=488 [accessed 3 November 2019]

23 Most commentators agree that this the author of the Song of Songs was not alluding to a botanical rose, but one of several spring flowers of the Palestine Hills, including the narcissus, lily, crocus and anemone.

24 Thomas the Cistercian, a 12th century monk, interpreted the Bridegroom as Christ seeking the Church as his Bride. See: Catherine Rose Cavadini, *The Commercium of the Kiss Who Saves: A Study of Thomas the Cistercian's Commentary on the Song of Songs* https://curate.nd.edu/show/nk322b9125m [accessed October 26, 2018.]

25 Wilkins, p. 113.

26 Anne Winston-Allen, *Gardens of Earthly and Heavenly Delight, Medieval Gardens of the Imagination:* (Helsinki: Modern Language Society, Neuphilologische Mitteilungen), Vol. 99, 1 (1998), p. 85. http://www.jstor.org/stable/43346182 [accessed October 26, 2018.]

27 Winston-Allen, *Stories of the Rose*, p.1.

28 Winston-Allen, p. 104.

29 Lisa Cucciniello, *Rose to Rosary*, in *Rose Lore*, ed. by Frankie Hutton, (Maryland: Lexington Books, 2015), p. 151.

30   See René Guénon, *The Esoterism of Dante* (Hillsdale, New York: Sophia Perennis, 1996).

31   Painton Cowen, *The Rose Window: Splendour & Symbol,* (London: Thames and Hudson Ltd., 2005), p. 27.

32   Titus Burckhardt, *Chartres and the Birth of the Cathedral*, (Bloomington, Indiana: World Wisdom Books, 2010), p.112.

33   Arthur Green, *The Heart of the Matter: Studies in Jewish Mysticism and Theology* (Lincoln: University of Nebraska Press, 2015), p. 81.

34   Arthur Edward Waite, *The Real History of the Rosicrucians,* (New York: J. W. Bouton, 1900), p. 16.

35   Emma Clark, *The Art of the Islamic Garden*, (Marlborough, UK: Crowood Press, 2011), p.34.

36   Idries Shah, *The Sufis*, (London: Octagon Press, 1999), p. 223.

37   Annemarie Schimmel, *The Celestial Garden in Islam*, ed. by Elisabeth B. MacDougall and Richard Ettinghausen, (Washington, D.C.: Dumbarton Oaks, Trustees for Harvard University, 1976), p. 39.

38   Inayat Khan, *The Sufi Message of Hazrat Inayat Khan, Vol. X,* (London: 1982).

39   Schimmel, p. 36.

40   Jelaluddin Rumi, *Call to Love: In the Rose Garden with Rumi*, ed./trans. by Andrew Harvey, (New York: Sterling Publishing Company, 2007).

41   Andrew Harvey, *Teachings of Rumi* (Boulder, Co.: Shambhala Publications, 1999), p. 114.

42   Harvey, *Teachings of Rumi*, p. 2.

43   Rumi

44   Rumi

45   Harvey, *Teachings of Rumi*, p. 3.

46   Rumi

47   Yunus Emre, *The Drop that Became the Sea: Lyric Poems of Yunus Emre* (Boulder: Shambhala Publications, 1989), p. 46.

48   Schimmel, 39.

49   Titus Burckhardt, *Alchemy: Science of the Cosmos, Science of the Soul*, (London: J.M.Watkins Ltd.1967), p. 28.

50   A. E. Waite, *The Brotherhood of the Rosy Cross,* (NewYork: University Books, *1924*), p. 97.

51   This is the reason the Rosicrucian rose is red, the sign of completion of the Great Work.

52   See McIntosh, *The Rosicrucians,* 59-60. Prof McIntosh draws some interesting parallels between Chinese Taoist and Western alchemy. He concludes: 'Given the sexual interpretation, many of the European alchemical texts seem to make sense' but also adds, 'Whether any

Europeans practised anything akin to Taoist alchemy is difficult to establish.'

53   Sir George Ripley, *The Bosome-Book,* http://www.levity.com/alchemy/bosom.html [accessed 19/10/18]

54   Jonathan Hughes, *Arthurian Myths and Alchemy*, (Stroud, UK, Sutton Publishing, 2002), p. 307.

55   Rudolf Steiner, *The Secret Stream: Christian Rosenkreutz and Rosicrucianism: Selected Lectures and Writings,* (New York: Steiner Books), p. 104.

56   McIntosh, Christopher and McIntosh, Donate Pahnke, *Fama Fraternitatis*, (CreateSpace Independent Publishing Platform, 2014), p. 45.

57   Christopher McIntosh, *The Rosicrucians: The History, Mythology, and Rituals of an Esoteric Order*, (York Beach, Maine: S. Weiser, 1997), p. 27.

58   Christopher McIntosh, *The Rosicrucian Dream*, in Jay Kinney, ed. *The Inner West: An Introduction to the Hidden Wisdom of the West.* (New York: Jeremy P. Tarcher/Penguin, 2004), p. 200.

59   Christopher McIntosh, and Donate Pahnke McIntosh, p. 49.

60   Tobias Churton, *The Invisible History of the Rosicrucians: The World's Most Mysterious Secret Society*, (Rochester, Vermont: Inner Traditions, 2009), p. 190.

61   Lewis, H. Spencer, *The Rosy Cross and the Rosary*, http://rosicrucian.50webs.com/hsl/hsl-rosy-cross-and-the-rosary.htm. [Accessed September 30, 2018].

62   Although the author of this book is given as Joachim Frizius, modern scholars believe this was a pen name for Robert Fludd. Adam McLean has recently identified an earlier source for this emblem which makes for a fascinating comparison. See http://www.alchemywebsite.com/fludd_rose.html

63   Israel Regardie, et al, *The Golden Dawn: An Account of the Teachings, Rites and Ceremonies of the Order of the Golden Dawn, revised edition,* (Woodbury, Minnesota: Llewellyn Publications, 1986), p.38.

64   Israel Regardie, p.310.

65   Israel Regardie, p. 47.

66   A. E. Waite, *The Brotherhood of the Rosy Cross,* p. 92.

67   A. E. Waite, *Rosicrucian Rites and Ceremonies of the Fellowship of the Rosy Cross*, (Burnaby, BC, Canada: Ishtar Publishing), p. 14.

68   Waite, p. 136-7.

69   A.E. Waite, *The Pictorial Key to the Tarot,* (New York: University Books, 1966), p. 76.

70   Waite, p. 60.

71   Richard Ellman, *W. B. Yeats: The Man and the Masks,* (New York: W.W. Norton & Co., 1978), p.188.

72   W. B. Yeats, *The Letters of W. B. Yeats,* ed. by Allen Wade, (New York:

The Macmillan Company, 1955), p. 211.

73 W. B. Yeats, *Essays and Introductions,* (London: The Macmillan Press, 1974), p. 193.

74 Ellman, p. 94

75 A. N. Jeffares, *A New Commentary on the Poems of W.B. Yeats,* (London: Palgrave Macmillan, 1984), p.20.

76 W. B. Yeats, *The Variorum Edition of the Poems of WB Yeats,* ed. by Peter Allt and Russell Alspach, (New York: Macmillan, 1957), p. 101.

77 Ellman, p.97

78 Yeats, *Variorum,* p. 101.

79 Yeats, *Essays and Introductions,* p. 255.

80 Yeats, *Variorum,* p. 811.

81 Yeats may have had a hand in the rose symbolism within Waite's tarot deck. In an article in the *Occult Review* (Volume X, 307-317) titled, *The Tarot: A Wheel of Fortune,* Waite stated that although he and Pamela Colman Smith designed the deck, 'we have had other help from one who is deeply versed in the subject.' Roger Parisious in *Figures in a Dance: W. B. Yeats and the Waite-Rider Tarot,* suggested that this help came from Yeats.

82 Yeats, *Variorum,* p. 174.

83 Yeats, *Variorum,* p. 812.

84 William Blake. *The Complete Poetry and Prose of William Blake,* ed. David V. Erdman, (New York, Doubleday, 1988), p. 18.

85 Yeats, *Variorum,* p. 812.

86 Ellman, p.120.

87 Yeats, *Essays and Introductions,* p.197.

88 Ellman, pp. 97-8.

89 Ellman, p.121.

90 Yeats, *Variorum,* p. 170.

91 W. B. Yeats, *Variorum,* p. 137.

92 Steven Putzel, *Reconstructing Yeats: The Secret Rose and The Wind Among the Reeds,* (Lanham: Rowman & Littlefield 1986), p. 67.

93 William B. Yeats, *Mythologies,* (New York: Scribner, 1959), p. 270

94 Yeats, *Mythologies,* p. 286

95 Yeats, *Mythologies,* p. 288

96 Yeats, *Mythologies,* p. 157. The epithet is a reference to Shelley's poem, *Hymn to Intellectual Beauty,* which is about ideal beauty as distinct from its earthly forms.

97 Yeats, *Mythologies,* pp.162-3.

98 Allen Grossman, *Poetic Knowledge in the Early Yeats,* (Charlottesville: University Press of Virginia, 1969), p. 50.

99 Yeats, *Mythologies,* p.283. The central portion of this passage was deleted in Yeats' final version of the story.

100 Yeats, *Mythologies,* p. 283.
101 See Mara Freeman, *Grail Alchemy: Initiation in the Celtic Mystery Tradition* (Rochester,Vermont: Inner Traditions, 2014).
102 Yeats, *Essays and Introductions*, pp. 151-2.
103 Sir Arthur Thomas Quiller-Couch, *The Oxford Book of Ballads,* (London: The Clarendon press, 1963), p. 4.
104 T. S. Eliot, *Collected Poems,* (London: Faber and Faber, 1979), p.97.
105 T. S. Eliot, *Four Quartets,* (London: Faber and Faber, Ltd.,) 1970, p.13.
106 Lyndall Gordon, *T.S. Eliot: An Imperfect Life*, (New York: W. W. Norton & Company, 2000), p. 123.
107 T. S. Eliot, *Collected Poems,* p. 234.
108 The Complete Poems and Plays of T. S. Eliot, (London: Faber and Faber, 2004), p. 171
109 T. S. Eliot, The Complete Poems, (London: Faber and Faber, 2004), p.171.
110 Elizabeth A. Drew, *T.S. Eliot, the Design of His Poetry,* (Oxfordshire: Taylor & Francis, 1950), p. 227.
111 T. S. Eliot, *Four Quartets,* p. 42.
112 T. S. Eliot, The Complete Poems, (London: Faber and Faber, 2004), p. 181.
113 T. S. Eliot, *Four Quartets,* p.47.
114 T. S. Eliot, *Four Quartets,* p. 48.

IMAGE CREDITS

Page 5.   Nguyen, Marie-Lan, 2009. 'Ludovisi Throne' marble relief of Birth of Aphrodite (disputed), 460 BCE [Online]. San Francisco: Wikimedia Foundation. Available from: https://commons.wikimedia.org/wiki/Category:Ludovisi_Throne [Accessed August 22, 2022].

Page 6.   IanDagnall Computing / Alamy Stock Photo, 2017. *The Birth of Venus* by Sandro Botticelli (Alessandro di Mariano di Vanni Filipepi, c.1487. Uffizi Gallery, Florence, Italy.

Page 9.   Museum of Naples, 2018. *Flora or Allegory of Spring*, [Online]. San Francisco: Wikimedia Foundation. Stabiae (Castellammare die Stabia), Villa (di) Arianna, cubiculum w 26 - museum / inventory number: Napoli, Museo Archeologico Nazionale 8834. Available from: https://commons.wikimedia.org/wiki/File:Wall_painting_-_Flora_-_Stabiae_(villa_di_Arianna)_-_Napoli_MAN_8834.jpg [Accessed 22 August 2022].

Page 13.   Peter Horree / Alamy Stock Photo, 2013. *Mummy Mask woman with a wreath of flowers.*

Page 16.   Chronicle / Alamy Stock Photo, 2010. *The Golden Ass* title page of a 16th century German edition.

Page 18.   Carole Raddato, 2014. Marble Statue of Isis with sistrum and situla from Villa Adriana, 1CE, Capitoline Museums, Rome [Online]. San Francisco: Wikimedia Foundation. Available from: https://commons.wikimedia.org/wiki/File:Marble_statue_of_Isis,_the_goddess_holds_a_situla_and_sistrum,_ritual_implements_used_in_her_worship,_from_117_until_138_AD,_found_at_Hadrian%27s_Villa_(Pantanello),_Palazzo_Nuovo,_Capitoline_Museums_(12945630725).jpg [Accessed 22 August 2022].

Page 19.   Lim, Edward, 2009. *Écusson avec rose et glaive, placé au plafond, à Rhodes,* [Online]. Available from: Sub rosa... | memento (diptyqueparis-memento.com) [Accessed 22 August 2022].

Page 27.   Science History Images / Alamy Stock Photo, 2017. *From Tacuinum Sanitatis,* 15th century, Lombardy. Biblioteca Casanatense, Rome, etc.

Page 31.   The Picture Art Collection / Alamy Stock Photo, 2013. *Das Paradiesgärtlein anagoria* by the Upper Rhenish Master, 15th century, Städel Museum, Frankfurt.

Page 39.   Unknown photographer. *Madonna of the Rose Garden* by Stefano da Zevio, Italy, 15th century, Castelvecchio Museum, Verona, [Online]. San Francisco: Wikimedia Foundation. Available from: https://commons.wikimedia.org/wiki/File:Michelino_da_besozzo_o_stefano_da_zevio,_madonna_del_roseto,_castelvecchio,_verona.jpg [Accessed 22 August 2022].

Page 40.   history_docu_photo / Alamy Stock Photo, 2020. *Dorothea of Caesarea with the Christ-child*, wood engraving, 1410. Location unknown.

Page 43.   The Picture Art Collection / Alamy Stock Photo. From *Adoration of the Magi* in the 15th century prayer-book, *Hours of Catherine of Cleves*. Morgan Library and Museum, New York.

Page 45.   Archive of Research in Archetypal Imagery, Library [CGJ XIII/4/20]. *Dante and Beatrice in the Heavenly Rose,* [Online]. Lib., Biblioteca Apostelica Vaticana; Cod. Urb. lat. 365. Available at: https://aras.org/records/5fm.053, [Accessed 22 August 2022].

Page 49.   Guillaume Piolle. Northern Rose Window of Chartres Cathedral, [Online]. San Francisco: Wikimedia Foundation. Available from: https://commons.wikimedia.org/wiki/File:Chartres_-_cath%C3%A9drale_-_rosace_nord.jpg [Accessed 22 August 2022].

Page 54.   North Wind Picture Archives / Alamy Stock Photo. Garden scene from *Roman de la Rose* (HarI. M.S. 4425), circa 1480. The British Library, London.

Page 62.   Science History Images / Alamy Stock Photo. *Babur supervising the laying out of the Garden of Fidelity.*

Page 65.   Photographer unknown. *The Rose of Muhammad* from the Turkish manuscript *Akhlaq-I Rasul Allah*, Turkey 1708, Staatsbibliothek zu Berlin Ms. or. oct. 1602, 48v.

Page 67.   http://www.asia.si.edu/collections/singleObject.cfm?ObjectId=25323, *Sa'di in a Rose Garden*, Mughal Dynasty, circa 1645, Freer Gallery of Art, Smithsonian, Washington D.C. [Online]. San Francisco: Wikimedia Foundation. Available from: File:Mughal Dynasty, Sa'di in a Rose Garden, Reign of Emperor Shah Jahan, early 16th century, repainted 1645.jpg - Wikimedia Commons [Accessed 22 August 2022].

Page 77. Speckner, Rolf, 2008. *Atalanta Fugiens, Emblem XLII.JPG* by Michael Maier, Frankfurt 1618. Buch *Atalanta Fugiens*. [Online]. San Francisco: Wikimedia Foundation. Available from: https://commons.wikimedia.org/wiki/File:M.Maier._Atalanta_Fugiens._1618._Emblem_XLII.JPG [Accessed 22 August 2022].

Page 81. Mclean, Adam, 1999 – 2010. Emblem 6 by Mylius Domum, [Online]. Mylius version of 'Donum Dei' series coloured (alchemywebsite.com) [Accessed 22 August 2022].

Page 82. Mclean, Adam, 1999 – 2010. Emblem 3 by Mylius Domum, [Online]. Mylius version of 'Donum Dei' series coloured (alchemywebsite.com) [Accessed 22 August 2022].

Page 84. Archive of Research in Archetypal Imagery. *The Alchemical Red and White Rose*, Lubeck, Germany, Artist Unknown, from *The Magic Myth* by Joseph Campbell, Princeton University Press, 1974, pl/225, p.254. British Library, London, [Online]. Available at: https://aras.org/records/5go.681 [Accessed 22 August 2022].

Page 86. Nourse, R.S. King Arthur's Round Table at Winchester Castle - Winchester, Hampshire, England. [Online]. San Francisco: Wikimedia Foundation. Available from: https://commons.wikimedia.org/wiki/File:King_Arthur%27s_Round_Table_at_Winchester_Castle,_Winchester,_Hampshire,_England.png [Accessed 22 August 2022].

Page 97. Olaf Tausch, Relief im Tempel Ramses II. in Abydos, Ägypten. San Francisco: Wikimedia Foundation. Available from: https://commons.wikimedia.org/wiki/File:Abydos_Tempelrelief_Ramses_II._26.JPG Accessed 17 December, 2022].

Page 99. Frater5, 2007. Illustration of Rosy Cross symbol from 19th-century occult/mystical work, [Online]. San Francisco: Wikimedia Foundation. Available from: https://en.wikipedia.org/wiki/Rose_Cross#/media/File:Rosycross-Tetragrammaton.svg [Accessed 22 August 2022].

Page 102. 'Harmonious Conception of the Light of Nature' in *Secret Symbols of the Rosicrucians* by unknown 18th century German compiler.

Page 105. Engraving from Robert Fludd, *Summum bonum*, Frankfurt 1629. Coloured by Adam McLean. [Online]. Available from: https://

www.alchemywebsite.com/bookshop/Rosicrucian06.html
[Accessed 17 December, 2022].

Page 112. Golden Dawn Floor and Ceiling of Vault of the Adepts. [Online]. Available from http://ayay.co.uk/background/ esoteric_and_occult/golden_dawn_magic/seven-pointed-floor-and-ceiling-symbols-from-the-golden-dawn-vault-of-adepts/ [Accessed 22 August 2022].

Page 114. Fuzzipeg, 2008. Golden Dawn Rose Cross Lamen [Online]. San Francisco: Wikimedia Foundation. Available from: https://commons.wikimedia.org/wiki/File:Rose_Cross_Lamen.svg [Accessed 22 August 2022].

Page 120. The Fool, Rider-Waite tarot card [Online]. Available from: https://pixabay.com/illustrations/the-fool-tarot-major-arcana-6154764/ [Accessed 22 August 2022].

Page 121. The Magician, Rider-Waite tarot card [Online]. Available from: https://pixabay.com/illustrations/the-magician-tarot-major-arcana-6154763/ [Accessed 22 August 2022].

Page 121. The Empress, Rider-Waite tarot card [Online]. Available from: https://pixabay.com/illustrations/the-empress-tarot-major-arcana-6154768/ [Accessed 22 August 2022].

Page 122. Strength, Rider-Waite tarot card [Online]. Available from: https://pixabay.com/illustrations/strength-tarot-major-arcana-6154776/ [Accessed 22 August 2022].

Page 123. Death, Rider-Waite tarot card [Online]. Available from: https://pixabay.com/illustrations/tarot-major-arcana-death-13-card-6249972/ [Accessed 22 August 2022].

Page 133. Tate, Paul / Adobe Stock. McDermott's Castle island at sunrise in summer, Lough Key, Ireland.

Page 142. Photograph from Columbia.edu. Cover of W. B. Yeats's book, *The Secret Rose*, designed by Althea Gyles, 1897, [Online]. San Francisco: Wikimedia Foundation. Available from: https://commons.wikimedia.org/wiki/File:The_Secret_Rose,_1897,_cover_by_Althea_Gyles.JPG [Accessed 22 August 2022].

Page 145. https://www.flickr.com/photos/nationallibrarynz_commons/15811959151, 2014. Cover of W. B. Yeats' book, *Poems*, 1912, designed by Althea Gyles, [Online]. San Francisco: Wikimedia Foundation. Available from: https://commons.wikimedia.org/wiki/File:YEATS(1912)_Poems(15811959151).jpg [Accessed 22 August 2022].

Page 147. Merlin Prints. *Riders of the Sidhe,* by John Duncan, 1911. [Online]. McManus Gallery, Dundee. San Francisco: Wikimedia Foundation. Available from: File:Riders of the Sidhe.jpg -

Wikimedia Commons [Accessed 22 August 2022].

Page 148. Lytvynovych Levgeniia . Hawthorn, iStock photos, May 20, 2020

Page 148. Vorontsova, Marina. Medical plant dog rose, Dreamstime stock photos.

Page 150. Herbert McNair, *Tamlaine*.

Page 162. Jonathan Buckley, The National Trust Photolibrary / Alamy Stock Photo. The Rose Garden in June at Sissinghurst.

Page 166. Hans Kyoto. *pink lotus flowers blooming in the pool*. [Online]. San Francisco: Wikimedia Foundation. Available from: https://commons.wikimedia.org/wiki/File:7618944x.jpg [Accessed 17 December, 2022].

Page 169. Historic Illustrations/ Alamy Stock Photo, 2020. Dante and Beatrice gaze upon the highest Heaven, Paradiso.

Page 171. Lambert, David, 2008. Thomas Stearns Eliot memorial. Westminster Abbey, London, England.

Mara Freeman, M.A. is a British author of Western esoteric spirituality which she has been teaching for over thirty years. Her best-selling book, *Kindling the Celtic Spirit* (Harper, 2001), has been hailed as the finest modern introduction to Celtic spirituality and its relevance to us today. This was followed by *Grail*  *Alchemy* (Inner Traditions, 2014), which has been called 'a literary temenos of our time, a sacred space, in which to further explore one's own inner journey'.

For many years she contributed extensively to *Parabola, the Journal of Myth and Tradition*, and she is the writer of the popular annual calendar, *Sacred Celtic Sites* (Amber Lotus, Portland, Or.). While living in California for many years, Mara gave lectures and taught experiential workshops throughout the United States. This led to a 20-year adventure taking groups on transformational tours, pilgrimages and retreats to ancient and sacred sites of Britain, Ireland and France.

Mara also founded the Avalon Mystery School, a three-year training programme in the Arts of Sacred Magic, which has students from all over the world. A qualified psychologist, astrologer, and psychic, she offers personal consultations in the Irish tradition of *Anamcara*, or Soul Guidance. Mara now divides her time between the hallowed bournes of Glastonbury and West Wales and delights in walking over the moors and by the sea, as well as working in her wild woodland garden.

To find out more about Mara's work, visit her website:
www.chalicecentre.net